TEA

TEACHING SECONDARY MUSIC

Edited by

Jayne Price and Jonathan Savage

Los Angeles | London | New Delhi
Singapore | Washington DC

First published 2012

SAGE Publications Ltd
1 Oliver's Yard
55 City Road
London EC1Y 1SP

SAGE Publications Inc.
2455 Teller Road
Thousand Oaks, California 91320

SAGE Publications India Pvt Ltd
B 1/I 1 Mohan Cooperative Industrial Area
Mathura Road
New Delhi 110 044

SAGE Publications Asia-Pacific Pte Ltd
33 Pekin Street #02-01
Far East Square
Singapore 048763

Library of Congress Control Number: 2011921546

British Library Cataloguing in Publication data

A catalogue record for this book is available from the British Library

ISBN 978-0-85702-393-3
ISBN 978-0-85702-394-0 (pbk)

Typeset by C&M Digitals (P) Ltd, Chennai, India
Printed in India at Replika Press Pvt Ltd
Printed on paper from sustainable resources

CONTENTS

LIST OF ABBREVIATIONS

AfL Assessment for Learning
CRB Criminal Records Bureau
DCSF Department for Children, Schools and Families
D&T Design and Technology
DfE Department for Education
GCSE General Certificate of Secondary Education
ICT Information and Communication Technology
INSET In-Service Training
MIDI Musical Instrument Digital Interface
NAME National Association of Music Educators
PAT Portable Appliance Testing
PGCE Post-Graduate Certificate of Education
PLTS Personal, Learning and Thinking Skills
PSHE Personal, Social and Health Education
Ofsted Office for Standards in Education
QCA Qualifications and Curriculum Authority
QCDA Qualifications and Curriculum Development Agency
QCF Qualifications and Credit Framework
SEAL Social and Emotional Aspects of Learning
VLE Virtual Learning Environment

ABOUT THE EDITORS

Jayne Price is the Music Education Coordinator, MTL Course Leader and MA tutor in the School of Education and Professional Development at the University of Huddersfield. She taught for 15 years as a music teacher and Head of Music in secondary schools in Derbyshire and Leeds and as CPD Coordinator with responsibility for the training and development budget. She has a particular interest in the early professional development of teachers and her work on the MA is closely linked to this area. She was the Lead Regional Subject Advisor for Music in the National Curriculum in Yorkshire and the Humber.

Jonathan Savage is a Reader in Education at the Institute of Education, Manchester Metropolitan University and Visiting Research Fellow to the Royal Northern College of Music. He has a wide range of interests related to teaching and educational research. He is Managing Director of UCan.tv, a not-for-profit company that produces educational software and hardware including Sound2Picture, Sound2Game and Hand2Hand. Jonathan also works as an educational consultant for CfBT, NAME, Roland UK, the TDA and other industrial partners. Jonathan maintains a blog (http://www.jsavage.org.uk) and free educational resources (http://www.ucan.me.uk).

ABOUT THE CONTRIBUTORS

Anthony Anderson is the subject leader for Music and an AST at Beauchamp College, Leicestershire. He was Lead Regional Subject Advisor for the East Midlands for Music in the National Curriculum. He writes regularly for Rhinegold and is music curriculum consultant for Espresso Education and Channel 4 Learning.

David Ashworth is a freelance education consultant, specialising in music technology. He is Project Leader for www.teachingmusic.org.uk and ICT consultant for *Musical Bridges.* Other recent work has included consultancy for Musical Futures, Trinity/OU, QCDA, BBC and Teachers TV, and CPD design and delivery for SSAT and many LEAs and music services. He is currently leading a number of projects in the North West of England and elsewhere on the use of ICT in live performance.

Carolyn Cooke is a subject leader for the Open University Music PGCE course. Prior to this she was Head of Music in a large secondary school and a Regional Subject Advisor for Music in the National Curriculum in the South East.

Martin Fautley is Professor of Education at Birmingham City University. For many years he was a secondary school teacher, subsequently undertaking doctoral research at Cambridge University into the teaching, learning and assessment of creative acts in the classroom. His research interests encompass creativity, composing music, assessment, activity theory, and teaching and learning in the arts. He has published academic research articles in *Music Education Research*, *British Journal of Music Education* and *Music Education International*.

Jane Humberstone is an Advanced Skills Teacher for the East Sussex Music Service and Secondary Curriculum Chair for the National Association of Music Educators, and was the South East Lead Regional Subject Adviser for Music in the National Curriculum. She has also engaged with and delivered INSET for the KS3 Music Programme, Exemplification of Standards and Assessing Pupil Progress. In her previous school (an 11–16 Performing Arts College) she was responsible for the implementation of Assessment for Learning.

Phil Kirkman lectures on the Music PGCE course at the University of Cambridge and teaches at secondary level in a comprehensive school in Suffolk. After several years of teaching and in management at secondary schools he moved into educational research and continues to work in areas relating to music teaching and learning, new educational technologies, compositional development and learner agency.

Kevin Rogers has been County Inspector with Hampshire Music Service for the past ten years, including a secondment to the Secondary National Strategy in 2005/2006 to lead on the KS3 music programme. He has also worked recently with QCDA on two national assessment projects involving music at KS3.

Alex Timewell is a passionate musician and general enthusiast for anything to do with music. Alex has worked for more than ten years as a Lecturer in Music and Performance Skills at a large UK further education college and is conducting a research project in music education for his PhD.

INTRODUCTION

Welcome to this book on music education. We hope you will find it an interesting and helpful collection of ideas about music and how it can best be taught in our schools.

This book is published at an interesting time. Under the previous Labour government, a series of curriculum reforms took place which asserted the primacy of the National Curriculum in all state schools. Music was a key part of these reforms, and a new statement about music and its place in the education of all our young people was central to this. As a curriculum subject, Music was included in this National Curriculum and, consequently, was an entitlement for all pupils and an essential element in their schooling from the ages of 5 to 14.

Today's political climate is more uncertain. The new Conservative and Liberal Democrat coalition is reconsidering the role and function of a National Curriculum. Already, the proposed free schools and new academies are exempt from following the National Curriculum. The recent publication of the White Paper (DfE 2010) called The Importance of Teaching has confirmed a number of things in this respect; it has set out a series of proposals and allows us, probably for the first time, to get a clear idea of where things are heading.

This has been a worrying period of time for music education. It is currently under a governmental review, being led by Darren Henley. So, it is interesting to examine this White Paper to see what, if any, conclusions can be drawn about music and its place within the school curriculum. Whatever the recommendations of the Henley review, they will have to fit within this broader policy framework.

Firstly, there is going to be another revision of the National Curriculum. Despite 2010–11 being the first academic year when the whole of Key Stage 3 is being taught the current version of the National Curriculum for the first time, the Coalition has made a clear decision that this is not fit for purpose.

When it comes to the primary and secondary curriculum, the general theme of the White Paper is to reduce what the Coalition sees as unnecessary prescription, bureaucracy and central control. Their view is that the National Curriculum in its current form weighs teachers down and saps their ability to be innovative and creative.

So, the White Paper proposes to review the National Curriculum over the next year or so, leading to the implementation of a new National Curriculum in September 2012. The next generation of the National Curriculum will set out 'clearly the core knowledge and understanding that all children should expected to acquire in the course of their schooling' (see DfE 2010: para. 4.7). Part of this revision will be a greater focus on subject content (ibid., para. 4.9). The final documentation will be 'slim, clear and authoritative (ibid., para. 4.12). At this point, it mentions that parents should be able to use its contents to hold schools to account.

The establishment of an English Baccalaureate has a prominent place in the White Paper. This will be awarded to students who secure 'good GCSE or iGCSE passes in English, mathematics, the sciences, a modern or ancient foreign language and a humanity such as history or geography'. None of the arts subjects have been included within this framework.

Early indications seem to be that head teachers will be keen to develop this award as there will be a separate record of the number of pupils getting this new award in new, published performance tables. Those schools that, in the words of the White Paper, 'succeed in giving their pupils a properly rounded academic education' will be more easily identified (ibid., para. 4.22). Arts subjects clearly fall outside this boundary. The White Paper does not say that they are not part of an academic education but, by omission, one can see that the view is that the arts are clearly not thought of as academic or worthy of inclusion. At Key Stage 4, there is a prescription in the White Paper that schools will be encouraged to offer 'a broad set of academic subjects to age 16, by introducing the English Baccalaureate'. Well, as we have seen already, music is clearly not conceptualised as an academic subject in this White Paper nor is it, or any of the arts, within the Baccalaureate. There are real dangers that this will lead to a reduction in music courses provided at Key Stage 4.

One of the few (three) references to music in the White Paper may be found at para 4.31. Here it is in full:

> Children should expect to be given a rich menu of cultural experiences. So we have commissioned Darren Henley to explore how we can improve music education and have more children learning to play an instrument. The Henley Review will also inform our

> broader approach to cultural education. We will support access to live theatre, encourage the appreciation of the visual and plastic arts and work with our great museums and libraries to support their educational mission.

Music, it seems, will form part of a cultural 'package' within the curriculum. It seems highly likely that Music will loose its place as a separate and discrete subject with the curriculum. It will be left to individual schools to decide how and when it is offered and to whom. From other comments made by the Secretary of State for Education in interviews on various media outlets immediately after the launch of the White Paper, it seems that he is imagining that schools will spend 50 per cent of their time on the National Curriculum subjects, with the other 50 per cent being at the discretion of the school. An uncharitable view could be that no prescription for music within the Key Stage 3 curriculum leads to no entitlement and no coherent, systematic and developmental progression for every child's music education. However, there is much to be decided and future policy announcements in 2011 will clarify this situation further.

Finally, additional worries about a two-tier system are still very prevalent. As we see in 4.14, academies and free schools will have the freedom not to follow the National Curriculum at all 'where they consider it appropriate' not to do so, but they will be required to teach a 'broad and balanced' curriculum. But this phrase, although having a historical resonance, is not defined. Many anticipate that this will lead to many children not receiving any music education at all within their compulsory schooling.

Trying to second guess these political changes is difficult. Similarly, pinning one's colours to any specific political 'mask' is unhelpful in a book like this. Rather, we (that is the editors and the individual chapter authors) have tried to produce a practical, and at times personal, account of how music should be taught and learnt within in our schools. In our view, this starts with the work of the teacher. Interestingly, recent initiatives in music have often prioritised the student or 'learner' and put them in a central position within formal educational settings. There is much of value in such approaches. But, fundamentally, we believe that it is the teacher who has the ultimate say in where teaching and learning within a formal educational setting such as a classroom begins. They have a choice to make. Formal, didactic teaching may be at one end of that spectrum; informal, student-led learning at the other. Either way, the choice is one that that the teacher has to make. Even not making an 'apparent' choice (and allowing students to decide) is, ultimately, a choice by the teacher in this respect.

So, what follows is a model for teaching and learning in music that is loosely based around the current National Curriculum for Music. Perhaps you are wondering why, given the current political uncertainly outlined above, we have chosen to use the National Curriculum framework for Music as a structure for this book? If, as seems possible, this framework may be removed or significantly slimmed down in forthcoming changes to the National Curriculum, why use it here at all?

These are good questions but there are good answers. Firstly, we believe that the current National Curriculum for Music provides a sound and comprehensive basis for successful teaching and learning in music. The majority of the authors in this book, including both of the editors, had no part to play in the construction of this framework. However, we believe that it presents a coherent and extremely helpful outline. The latest version of the National Curriculum published in 2007 built on the previous revision of 2000. This, in turn, was a helpful re-examination of the curriculum devised and implemented in the early 1990s. So, there is a strong historical tradition to the ideas and approaches inherent with the National Curriculum that we ignore at our peril.

Secondly, the National Curriculum orders present a systematic approach to teaching and learning in music within a broader curriculum framework that links other subjects, themes and ideas together in a holistic manner. While cross-curricular or inter-disciplinary approaches (and these are quite distinct) may seem a step beyond the main purpose of this book, we will argue in what follows that maintaining a broader perspective relating to music and its place within a child's education should be an essential aspect of every teacher's work.

Thirdly, all the writers within this book have seen the benefits in the teaching and learning of music that this framework has had on teachers working with it over the last few years. They were all part of a curriculum development project run by the National Association of Music Educators and CfBT Education Trust. This project supported the work of music teachers across the United Kingdom in numerous ways. By working closely with teachers, through large training events to one-to-one support in the planning of individual units of work, we have seen how the ideas contained within the National Curriculum for Music can be usefully applied to help broaden the ways that music can be best taught within our classrooms.

If you are someone who is just about to embark on a career in the teaching of music in our schools, or if you are an established teacher of music, we are sure that you will find plenty of value in the following pages. We are not arrogant enough to say that all the answers are here, but there is plenty of experience here to learn from. We trust that you will be open and receptive to new ideas. No one is the perfect teacher and we are all still learning. These ideas are offered in that spirit of shared discovery. In the words of an African proverb:

> If you want to go fast go alone,
> If you want to far go together.

References

Department for Education (2010) *The Importance of Teaching*. London: DFE. Also available online at: http://publications.education.gov.uk/default.aspx?PageFunction=productdetails&PageMode=publications&ProductId=CM+7980 (last accessed 15 December 2010).

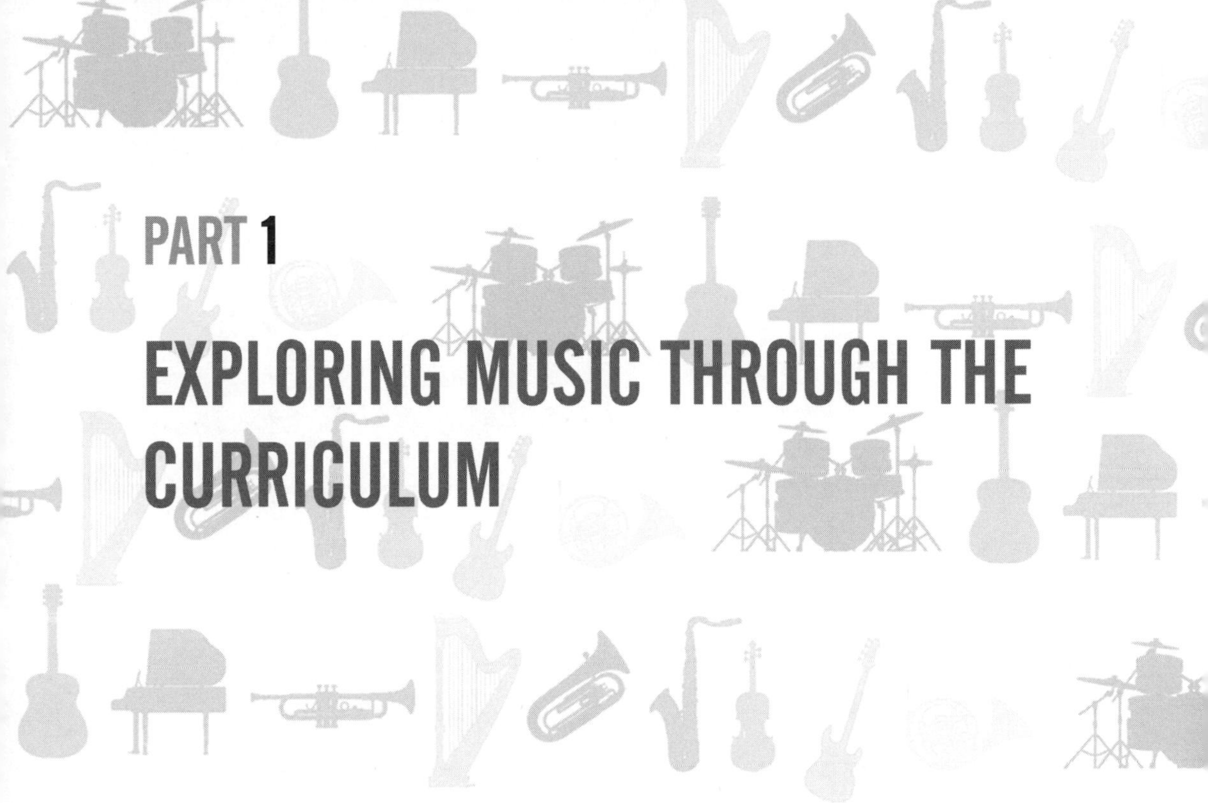

PART 1

EXPLORING MUSIC THROUGH THE CURRICULUM

This section considers the key curriculum frameworks that music should be taught through. These include Key Concepts and Key Processes (the focus of Chapters 1 and 2). Chapter 3 explores the ways in which a cross-curricular approach to teaching and learning in music can be beneficial. Chapter 4 considers how functional skills and personal, learning and thinking skills can be taught through meaningful musical experiences.

CHAPTER 1

THE KEY CONCEPTS FOR MUSICAL TEACHING

Jonathan Savage

Music for all

We believe that the study of music should be a central part of every child's education. This opening chapter explores some of the reasons for this statement in light of recent changes to the National Curriculum in the United Kingdom. It argues for an approach to music education that is built around young people being actively involved in their learning. It will focus on five key themes or concepts that all music educators, whether working in a school, community or instrumental setting, could apply to their teaching and use to help plan a quality experience for their students.

Why should music be for all?

One of the major changes to the last version of the National Curriculum has been the writing of an 'Importance Statement' for each subject. These statements capture the intrinsic value of their subjects and present these benefits for young people in a very helpful way. Each importance statement is related to the overall curriculum aims for all young people to become:

- successful learners who enjoy learning, make progress and achieve;
- confident individuals who are able to live safe, healthy and fulfilling lives;
- responsible citizens who make a positive contribution to society.

The first paragraph of the Importance Statement for Music reads as follows:

> Music is a unique form of communication that can change the way pupils feel, think and act. Music forms part of an individual's identity and positive interaction with music can develop pupils' competence as learners and increase their self-esteem. Music brings together intellect and feeling and enables personal expression, reflection and emotional development. As an integral part of culture, past and present, music helps pupils understand themselves, relate to others and develop their cultural understanding, forging important links between home, school and the wider world. (QCA 2007: 179)

This statement provides vital elements that justify music's place as a core part of any curriculum. Note the emphasis on its uniqueness, the role it plays as a key element in the development of a young person's emotional, physical and social development, the historical and cultural imperatives that have driven (or been driven by) music's impact on our world, and the ways it which music can provide a link between an individual and the wider world. For all these reasons (and perhaps many more that you can think of), music is a vital part of every child's early educational experiences.

But the Importance Statement for Music continues. A second paragraph begins to outline the particular benefits of a music education.

> Music education encourages active involvement in different forms of music-making, both individual and communal, helping to develop a sense of group identity and togetherness. Music can influence pupils' development in and out of school by fostering personal development and maturity, creating a sense of achievement and self-worth, and increasing pupils' ability to work with others in a group context. Music learning develops pupils' critical skills: their ability to listen, to appreciate a wide variety of music, and to make judgements about musical quality. It also increases self-discipline, creativity, aesthetic sensitivity and fulfilment. (QCA 2007: 179)

This paragraph begins to apply the foundational ideas about music and its importance outlined in the opening paragraph within the context of a music education. These sentences emphasise several key words that will become important themes throughout this book. Firstly, note the phrase 'active involvement'. Music is best taught and learnt through a process of active participation within its different forms or processes. Also, note the references to individual and group identity and a sense of togetherness. The positive enhancement of these attributes is a particularly important consideration for music teachers. Finally, the last two sentences of the importance statement make reference to a range of further skills that a quality music education can enhance in all students.

This important statement does, for all the authors whose work is featured in this book, exemplify the intrinsic benefits of a music education for all students in a very helpful way. We are used to hearing about the external, extrinsic benefits of a music education, e.g. learning a musical instrument helps you concentrate better, do better at mathematics, improve your literacy skills (BBC 2010). But how often can you recall the intrinsic value of a music education being promoted in discussions about education recently? This provides an excellent starting point and one that all music educators should be familiar with. Over the next few years it seems likely that music will need to fight its corner as a curriculum subject in our schools. Indeed, at the time of writing a new White Paper has been released (DfE 2010) and it seems highly likely that music will not feature as a subject within the National Curriculum from 2013. Be prepared to promote the intrinsic benefits of a music education for all at every opportunity!

The discussion so far has dwelt on some key justifications for music and music education. Perhaps you are wondering how this will effect or relate to your own emerging, or established, music teaching. As part of our work with the National Association of Music Educators (NAME) we were asked to try and describe what a compelling learning experience in music would be like. This took some of the key ideas of the Importance Statement and applied them, together with the Key Concepts (see below) into a practical statement about the characteristics of effective teaching and learning in music. The following statement represents our combined viewpoint. We are not holding this up as the answer! There may well be things here that you disagree with. Rather, we hope that you will want to think about it, unpick it and apply it to your own thinking about how you teach music.

For us, a compelling learning experience in music …

> … involves engaging with, enjoying and understanding music in ways that create meaning for each individual pupil. Music should be taught in ways that motivate and actively involve students, integrating the key processes of performing, composing, listening, reviewing and evaluating. The curriculum should allow pupils to personalise and take ownership of their learning experiences and encourage them to engage with and develop a broad range of knowledge, skills and understanding in a diversity of contexts.
>
> Music teachers need to be skilful, imaginative and enthusiastic. They will embody and demonstrate these musical processes in various ways. They should explore opportunities to build cross-curricular dimensions into their curriculum in a way that reflects the specific needs and interests of their students. In this way, music is enriched and has even greater relevance for pupils. Through creative exploration, learning should be underpinned by cultural and critical understanding, empowering all pupils to develop their senses of self-discipline, aesthetic sensitivity and fulfilment.
>
> Music activities should extend beyond the music department and permeate through the life of the school and local community. Compelling learning experiences in music become contextualised within pupils' own musical identities through encouraging them to participate in this rich network of school and community-centred musical activity.

The Key Concepts: the building blocks of a quality music education for all

While we guess that the majority of you who are reading this book will subscribe to the notion that a music education is important for all children, exactly how one should go about providing such an education is a matter of ongoing debate. Currently, there are significant and important voices calling for different approaches.

What would your essential components of a school, curriculum-based, music education for all be? It is worth dwelling on this question for a moment or two before reading on.

The most recent National Curriculum for Music was introduced to schools in 2008, although it has not been taught to the entirety of Key Stage 3 until 2010–11. It identifies five building blocks on which a comprehensive, curriculum-based music education should be built. In common with every other subject in the National Curriculum, these building blocks are called Key Concepts. They are:

- Integration of practice
- Cultural understanding
- Critical understanding
- Creativity
- Communication

Each Key Concept is defined in the Programme of Study and, for ease of reference, is quoted below.

> **1.1 Integration of practice**
>
> - Developing knowledge, skills and understanding through the integration of performing, composing and listening.
> - Participating, collaborating and working with others as musicians, adapting to different musical roles and respecting the values and benefits others bring to musical learning.
>
> **1.2 Cultural understanding**
>
> - Understanding musical traditions and the part music plays in national and global culture and in personal identity.
> - Exploring how ideas, experiences and emotions are conveyed in a range of music from different times and cultures.
>
> **1.3 Critical understanding**
>
> - Engaging with and analysing music, developing views and justifying opinions.
> - Drawing on experience of a wide range of musical contexts and styles to inform judgements.

1.4 Creativity

- Using existing musical knowledge, skills and understanding for new purposes and in new contexts.
- Exploring ways music can be combined with other art forms and other subject disciplines.

1.5 Communication

- Exploring how thoughts, feelings, ideas and emotions can be expressed through music.

(QCA 2007: 180–1)

Within this curriculum model, the Key Concepts become the essential building blocks of a music curriculum. Following on from the grand statements contained within the Importance Statement, they represent some concrete and practical ideas, or ways of thinking, about music education. Our argument throughout this book is that these Key Concepts are the starting point for planning opportunities for musical learning. As we will explore further in the following chapter, they are closely related to the Key Processes (which are the essential ways in which students should engage with the Key Concepts). Obviously, as with any kind of categorisation or schemata, there will be overlaps between various categories. But these Key Concepts are an essential tool so, for that reason, we will briefly take each in turn and explore what they mean.

Firstly, and perhaps most importantly, 'integration of practice' reinforces one of the central tenets of music education. The integration of the musical processes of performing, composing and listening (together with, in this curriculum model, the processes of reviewing and evaluating), undertaken both individually and collaboratively, underpin the development of musical knowledge, skills and understanding. These ideas have a long history. Swanwick's early work and ideas in books such as *Music, Mind and Education* (Swanwick 1988) have emphasised this holistic approach to teaching music. The precise learning processes within the music curriculum were contested in the very first National Curriculum, particularly in relation to the requirement for one, two or possibly three attainment targets (Swanwick 1992: 164–5). The holistic model of music education, where key processes are conceptualised as being fundamentally integrated, has won the day in the United Kingdom. Our model of music education is respected across the world to no small extent because of this. There is only one attainment target for music as a whole. The concept of a performance lesson without listening, or a composition lesson without reviewing and evaluating, is a misplaced one. First and foremost, teachers should ensure that the Key Processes of music education are taught in an integrated way.

Secondly, 'cultural understanding' provides a starting point for the music curriculum to explore how music functions in societies, both nationally and globally, and how this relates to personal identity and the development of positive relationships with others. While reading the Importance Statement, did you notice the significant emphasis placed on the individual student, their emerging identity and sense of self-esteem? This Key Concept provides the link between the individual student and their relationship to the wider musical world, whether that be in their physical local community or through a virtual community that spans the globe.

'Critical understanding' is the third Key Concept. It has much resonance with terminology such as 'responding and reviewing' and 'appraising' which were key pieces of terminology in the previous National Curriculum. The skills of musical analysis and aural perception which underpin the process of making judgements about music need to be taught systematically by teachers. The precise skills that these include are open to debate although some important ones are mentioned later in the curriculum orders. One skill, the ability to use staff notation, is a frequent source of contention among music educators. However, the important point here is to emphasise that topics such as music theory, analysis and perception all have a part to play in a rounded music education.

The fourth Key Concept is 'Creativity'. There are many views as to what the term 'creativity' in education really means. Here, the definition makes a significant play on using existing knowledge and skills in new contexts and for new purposes. It also places an emphasis on creative cross-curricular links (an idea we will explore further in Chapter 3). This leads us to an obvious point. Which other subjects have 'creativity' as a Key Concept and how do they define it? Discussions with colleagues from Art, Design and Technology and English will lead to some imaginative links being made between subjects that will help students considerably in contextualising their musical studies in the broader curriculum.

Finally, 'Communication' refers to how thoughts, feelings, ideas and emotions can be expressed through music. There are obvious links here to the third Key Concept of critical understanding.

Following the Key Concepts, the National Curriculum for Music presents the Key Processes. These will be the topic of discussion in Chapter 2. For now, the emphasis is rightly placed on these Key Concepts which should underpin and inform all of the curriculum choices and teaching approaches that you seek to adopt within your teaching. While the 'Range and Content' and 'Curriculum Opportunities' sections of the National Curriculum give you specific examples of the types of musical activities and approaches that you might seek to utilise (and there is a degree of choice there between what you choose and how much time you spend on each), at the level of Key Concepts there is no such ambiguity. These five Key Concepts are, in our view, rightly considered as the cornerstones of an effective, broad and balanced music education.

Summary

It is important to remember that the latest version of the National Curriculum for Music is designed as a benchmark. It sets out a core set of values and describes the essential types of musical learning that all students should experience. The Key Concepts represent the essential core of this experience and should be your starting point in considering how to plan for musical teaching and learning.

However, the curriculum as a whole can, and should, be treated flexibly. Across the whole of the Key Stage 3 curriculum, there is now less prescribed content and an increased focus on the Key Concepts. This means that, if you feel it is appropriate for your students' needs, you can teach music by using any one of a variety of methodologies, e.g. the methods of Kodaly, Dalcroze, Musical Futures or the Secondary Strategy. Teachers should use this new flexibility to design and develop their own curriculum models that best suit their particular situations and their learners.

Structure of the book

In what follows throughout this book we will explore some of this flexibility and give you examples of what a music curriculum might look like for your school. The book is structured in three main sections.

1. Exploring music through the curriculum (Chapters 1–4)

This section considers the key curriculum frameworks that music should be taught through. As we have seen, these include Key Concepts and Key Processes (the focus of Chapter 2). Chapter 3 explores the ways in which a cross-curricular approach to teaching and learning in music can be beneficial. Chapter 4 considers how functional skills and personal, learning and thinking skills can be taught through meaningful musical experiences.

2. Establishing music in the classroom (Chapters 5–9)

This section looks in greater detail at the Range and Content and the Curriculum Opportunities sections of the National Curriculum for Music, particularly focusing on those aspects which are new. The aim here is to explore how these aspects might be approached in practice. These chapters will outline examples and case studies and also recommend resources which are useful in helping teachers to implement these aspects of the curriculum.

Chapter 5 begins this process with the focus on musical performance. The challenge here is to provide a range of opportunities both in and outside the classroom for *all* students.

Chapter 6 explores the sociological impact of music, the role of the music industry and intellectual property rights. It demonstrates how these issues can be embedded in existing units of work and offer alternative ways of engaging students with these issues through digital technologies, role play and a range of resources being developed by industry partners.

While the use of technology has always featured in the music curriculum, the latest iteration of the National Curriculum emphasises the role of technology in musical performance. Chapter 7 focuses on a range of classroom activities which develop students' musical performance skills through digital technologies.

Opportunities to work with accomplished musicians who can model creative musical processes can be inspirational and motivating for students. However, this can be a difficult aspect of the curriculum to achieve with limited resources. Chapter 8 encourages you to consider different ways in which musicians can work within your classroom and provides a range of starting points to help teachers to develop these opportunities for students.

Finally in this section on establishing music in the classroom, in Chapter 9 the book turns to issues of musical leadership. Projects such as Musical Futures have shown that, when given the opportunity, students can become more independent in their music-making. This requires them to take responsibility for their learning and become musical leaders. Chapter 9 examines some of these approaches, and shows how performing and composing activities can be developed that facilitate musical leadership skills in a positive way.

3. Enriching musical models of development and assessment (Chapters 10–12)

The final section of the book explores three issues of significant importance to music teachers in recent years: musical development, assessment, and the broadening curriculum for students aged 14–19.

Chapter 10 focuses on how you can conceptualise and plan for musical understanding and development. Linking to a range of common frameworks, it suggests planning activities which will help you review your scheme of work in order to enhance the development of music understanding.

Assessment in music education can be problematic. Chapter 11 explores this topic in significant detail. While many of the processes outlined in the Assessment for Learning (AfL) strategy come naturally to music teachers, often they are under pressure to conform to excessive demands for data in schools which has led to a focus on 'AfL' based on a misunderstanding of the level descriptors. Ways of recognising and collecting evidence of progress will be explored and approaches to assessment in KS3 will be developed.

Within the context of exploring musical progression after KS3, the final chapter will outline approaches to teaching the 14–19 curriculum which focus on developing students as independent learners ready to take ownership of their music-making.

Reflective Questions

1. What is special about Music as a subject? Why do I think it is important for all children to study Music at school?
2. How can I begin to use the Key Concepts for Music in my planning of a unit of work at Key Stage 3?
3. What challenges has this chapter presented? How can I begin to change my own teaching practice in response to these challenges?

Further Reading 

Fautley, M. and Savage, J. (2007) *Creativity in Secondary Education*. Exeter: Learning Matters.
Swanwick, K. (1999) *Teaching Music Musically*. London: Routledge.

References

BBC (2010) 'Music tuition falling, poll suggests'. Online at: http://www.bbc.co.uk/news/education-11179448 (accessed 6 September 2010).

Department for Education (2010) *The Importance of Teaching: The Schools White Paper 2010*. London: DfE.

Qualifications and Curriculum Authority (2007) *Music: Programme of Study for Key Stage 3 and Attainment Target*. London: QCA.

Swanwick, K. (1988) *Music, Mind and Education*. London: Routledge.

Swanwick, K. (1992) 'Open peer commentary: musical knowledge: the saga of Music in the National Curriculum', *Psychology of Music*, 20(2): 162–79.

Swanwick, K. (1994) *Music, Mind and Education*. London: Routledge.

CHAPTER 2

THE KEY PROCESSES OF MUSICAL LEARNING

Jayne Price

Introduction

The five Key Processes outline the 'essential skills and processes which pupils need to learn in order to make progress across the subject' (QCA 2007: 182). In the National Curriculum for Music, these are divided into two aspects: (1) performing, listening and composing; and (2) reviewing and evaluating. As outlined earlier, however, it is essential that the Key Processes in music are seen as interrelated. Connections between all aspects are evident in the way that the processes are conceived and taught. For example, the reviewing and evaluating processes support the development and refinement of students' compositions and performances; students' listening skills are developed as they perform in ensemble with others; identifying conventions and contextual influences in music of different styles, genres and traditions helps students to make reasoned decisions when composing their own music. These examples demonstrate how the Key Concept of integration works in practice.

The carefully worded guidance in the Programme of Study makes it clear that students develop their musicianship and musical understanding by engaging in these skills and processes. In other words, they are a means to an end. This is an important concept to come to terms with as it underpins the

Programme of Study for music. Rather than technical competence, it is the depth and quality of the students' responses when performing composing, listening, reviewing and evaluating that are important in demonstrating their musicianship and musical understanding.

In this chapter, the Key Processes will be discussed in detail, with a particular focus on how these can be introduced and developed in the classroom in an integrated way. We will explore ways of increasing the level of challenge across the processes and make suggestions to ensure that understanding gained within the primary curriculum is built upon at secondary level.

What are the Key Processes?

The key performing processes are identified as follows:

- Sing in solo or group contexts developing vocal techniques and musical expression.
- Perform with control of instrument specific techniques and musical expression.
- Practise, rehearse and perform with awareness of the different parts, the roles and contributions of different members of the group, the audience and venue.

(QCA 2007: 182)

There is an obvious emphasis here on the development of instrumental and vocal skills, but the prominence of musical expression in the statements is significant, as this is one of the most important ways for students to demonstrate their musical understanding and musicianship. A 'musical' performance can be difficult to define, but we all know it when we hear it! By developing performing activities which allow students to develop their own interpretations, and by encouraging them to further refine and develop their initial attempts, students become more aware of aspects such as expression, articulation and phrasing, their own and others' parts within an ensemble, and how they can communicate more effectively with an audience.

It is imperative to give students a broad experience of performing in terms of the instruments and repertoire used. Students need to have opportunities to play a range of instruments when performing in order to develop a range of techniques and develop their ability to be expressive. Vocal techniques are identified in the widest sense by using the voice to make music in a variety of ways such as rapping, beatboxing, scat singing and chant. Group contexts include singing in unison and in parts.

It is important to note that elsewhere in the Programme of Study the importance of providing opportunities for students to perform in a range of contexts is outlined. These include opportunities:

- to perform both inside and outside of the classroom;
- to develop individual vocal and instrumental performing skills;
- to work individually, in small groups and as a class;
- to use music technologies to develop and enhance performances; and to work with a range of musicians

(QCA 2007)

As will be seen in later chapters, these activities broaden students' experience and help to develop their confidence when performing.

As we suggested earlier, we believe that learning appropriate musical theory is part of a rounded musical education and indeed the Programme of Study outlines that students should be able to use staff and other relevant notations. However, this should not dominate performing and composing activities in such a way that students end up giving a stifled performance because of their inability to read their part, or their compositions become simplistic and formulaic, limited by their ability to notate them. Being mindful of the context and traditions of the music studied is important here. For example, it is inappropriate to develop a solo section of a Samba piece by asking students to write an 8-bar phrase using crotchets and quavers. This will inevitably lead to an uninspiring and unconvincing performance that bears little resemblance to Samba!

The composing processes are:

- Create develop and extend musical ideas by selecting and combining resources within musical structures, styles, genres and traditions.
- Improvise, explore and develop musical ideas when performing.

(QCA 2007: 182)

The explanatory notes in the Programme of Study clarify 'creating, developing and extending musical ideas' by suggesting that activities could include composing original music, arranging existing musical ideas and creating new pieces using a range of existing material. This emphasis on the manipulation of existing musical material allows teachers to introduce a variety of stimulus material to students in order to practise their composing skills and develop their understanding of the devices, structures and elements used within specific styles, genres and traditions. The aim here is that as students progress, they begin to make their own creative decisions about the most appropriate musical resources and devices to use to create an intended effect. In order to encourage this we perhaps need to balance more directed composing tasks with activities which require a more creative response from students and which may generate unexpected outcomes.

Using abstract starting points for composition is one way of developing students' creative thinking further. In the example below, students used their understanding of motivic development, musical structure and harmony to compose innovative and highly original pieces.

In a Year 8 lesson, the teacher prepared a number of motivic ideas in an envelope that the students chose from at random. The students were asked to explore their motif and compose a musical fragment they were happy with. Once the students had explored the idea on their own, they joined with a partner to share their idea and choose one to develop further or perhaps put their ideas together. The students then joined with another pair to explore all the musical ideas further, and gradually they developed a composition, during which they were engaged in making complex musical decisions every step of the way. The resulting music was highly original and each piece was entirely different. The students enjoyed talking to each other about how they had developed their original ideas to complete the compositions.

The way that teachers intervene with this creative process is important: too much direction and the students begin to develop the teachers' ideas rather than their own, too little and some students may struggle to get started. In this lesson, careful questioning which encouraged students to justify their musical decisions and to consider alternatives helped the students to clarify their thought processes and encouraged their creative thinking. This intervention also enabled the teacher to offer appropriate challenges that enabled all students to succeed and to take a full and active part in the group composition.

Both of the composing processes imply that the intended outcome should be performing. This is obviously something that is well embedded in current practice in the classroom, and the decisions that students make during the composing process are guided by critical listening of how the piece sounds and deciding what works and what does not. Observing this process and talking to the students about their work, as well as listening to the final performance, will give teachers an insight into students' musical understanding and developing musicianship.

This emphasises why the listening processes are now linked more explicitly with the performing and composing processes. The listening processes are defined as:

- Listen with discrimination and internalise and recall sounds.
- Identify the expressive use of musical elements, devices, tonalities and structures.

(QCA 2007: 182)

Students should be given opportunities to listen to a wide range of music. In the Range and Content section of the Programme of Study, this is outlined as 'a range of live and recorded music from different times and cultures' and 'a range of classical and popular traditions and current trends in music that reflect cultural diversity and a global dimension' (QCA 2007: 183). This develops students' understanding of musical devices, processes and conventions, and helps them to make links between their own work and that of established composers.

The importance of listening has been emphasised frequently by Ofsted (2009). These latest findings outline how regular opportunities to listen to music from a wide variety of times and places can help students to make rapid progress in composition, as well as highlighting the importance of listening in developing musical intelligence. The report encourages teachers to explore the nature of music with students in order to increase their understanding.

> Pupils in Key Stage 3 were rarely enabled to achieve the highest levels because there was insufficient exploration of music as a living personal, social and cultural experience. Instead, the lessons seem focused on the nuts and bolts, such as which musical devices had been used but without exploring why. Formulaic rather than musical responses were the result. (Ofsted 2009: 47)

It is worth noting that one of the ways that Ofsted judge students' achievements and standards is through their understanding of how and why different kinds of music are created. Further judgement is made on whether the students engage positively with different kinds of music and have respect for different musical traditions (Ofsted 2009).

The listening processes are also linked closely to reviewing and evaluating. These processes are:

- Analyse, review, evaluate and compare pieces of music.
- Identify conventions and contextual influences in music of different styles, genres and traditions.
- Communicate ideas and feelings about music using expressive language and musical vocabulary to justify their opinions.
- Adapt their own ideas and refine and improve their own and others' work.

(QCA 2007: 102)

The reviewing and evaluating processes underpin the Key Concept of critical understanding. Students practise these skills in a variety of contexts:

- when they are developing and refining performances and compositions;
- when they make choices about the most appropriate musical elements, devices and structures to use in their own music;
- when they evaluate whether their pieces fulfil their intended purpose and effect;
- when they think about whether their pieces communicate their thoughts, feelings and emotions successfully to their audience.

These processes in particular have implications for the way in which we plan activities in the classroom. If students are to be given opportunities to adapt, refine and improve their own and others' work, we need to allow time for this to happen during the creative process rather than planning time for feedback just in the 'performing' or (even worse) the 'assessment' lesson.

Integrating the Key Processes

During the discussion so far we have emphasised the integrated nature of the Key Processes in music. The following case study further illustrates how this can happen in practice.

The unit of work for Year 8 focused on developing soundscapes using vocal techniques. The original stimulus material was the Honda Civic Choir advertisement composed by Steve Sidwell. The students watched and listened to the advert identifying how the vocal techniques, musical elements and devices were used to create the soundscape. The teacher explained how the composition was developed by first recording the car in as many different ways as possible, before exploring how these sounds could be recreated with voices. The class also discussed how the composer conducts and leads the performance of the piece and the ensemble skills displayed by the choir.

The teacher then led the students in a class performance of 'Train Rhythms' from *Voiceworks* (Block and Kempton 2001) before splitting the students into small ensemble groups to create their own arrangement of the piece. The teacher challenged the students to refine their performances by encouraging one student in each group to act as the 'conductor', controlling the dynamics, tempo, articulation and phrasing of their piece.

Students then watched Perpetuum Jazzile's performance of 'Africa' (available at http://www.youtube.com/watch?v=yjbpwlqp5Qw) and the teacher asked students to develop their own composition using vocal techniques and body percussion. The students were inspired and quickly developed their own ideas. One group created an arrangement of Rihanna's 'Umbrella', singing a capella, with the chorus accompanied by beatboxing and raindrop sounds. Another group found a recording of a coffee machine online and recreated it using vocal sounds.

When the students had got to the stage where they had developed an initial version of their piece, the teacher paired the groups together and asked the two groups to listen to each other's pieces and provide feedback to help each other to refine and develop their work. Afterwards, as students were rehearsing their own pieces again, the teacher encouraged them to think about the visual performance aspects of their piece and how they could communicate more successfully with the audience.

(Continued)

(Continued)

This sequence of lessons developed the following Key Processes:

- Sing in solo or group contexts developing vocal techniques and musical expression.
- Practise, rehearse and perform with awareness of the different parts, roles and contributions of different members of the group, the audience and venue.
- Create, develop and extend musical ideas by selecting and combining resources within musical structures, styles, genres and traditions.
- Listen with discrimination and internalise and recall sounds.
- Identify the expressive use of musical elements, devices, tonalities and structures.
- Analyse, review, evaluate and compare pieces of music.
- Adapt their own ideas and refine and improve their own and others' work.

The integration of performing, composing, listening, reviewing and evaluating should continue in the 14–19 curriculum in order to develop students' musical understanding further. There seems to be a temptation to separate the different aspects of GCSE and A-level syllabuses, perhaps to solve a resources problem or in an attempt to cover the theoretical and historical aspects needed to answer the listening paper. However, listening and analysis 'lessons' which divorce theoretical and practical aspects of music do little to help students truly understand complex musical concepts.

The following example shows how a teacher consolidated students' understanding of musical devices by integrating the musical processes in a GCSE lesson.

The lesson started with the teacher modelling the musical devices of imitation, call and response, riff, drone, ostinato, pedal and modulation on the piano. The students identified the musical device being demonstrated using whiteboards. The students explained their answers and, with careful questioning, the teacher encouraged them to extend and develop their answers, thinking about how and why these might be used in music.

The main task of the lesson was for the students to create a revision podcast outlining the musical devices. In small groups, the students were asked to compose a 30-second piece clearly exploiting one of the musical devices. As well as developing the composition, each group had to explain how they had used the device in their piece. The students were encouraged to develop the quality of their performances so as to enhance the revision resource.

Finally, students were asked to identify devices in a past listening paper question which the students did successfully. Subsequently the revision resource was made available on the school Virtual Learning Environment (VLE) and the students were encouraged to identify music they had listened to or were working on in their instrumental lessons which used the devices.

Making progress with the Key Processes

Much has been written about the overemphasis on increasing 'difficulty' when thinking about progression across the Key Processes (Ofsted 2009; Rogers 2009). This stems from a misunderstanding of how musical progress is defined in the National Curriculum and the level descriptors. The first sentences in the level descriptors exemplify the development of musical understanding over time, but if we are to develop students' ability to 'listen with discrimination and to internalise and recall sounds' across the Key Stage, we need to be able to conceptualise what this and all the other Key Processes might look like in Year 7, and what they will look like in Year 9.

The level descriptors suggest that when performing at level 4, students begin to identify and explore the relationship between sounds; they can play simple parts and maintain their own part within an ensemble, showing awareness of how the parts fit together. As they move on through the levels, they become more aware of their own role within ensemble performances, they begin to make adjustments to their own part when necessary to fit their part musically within the group, and they begin to make expressive use of musical devices and elements. By level 7 students have a much deeper understanding of musical style and can perform appropriately within given musical styles, genres and traditions. The most advanced performers reflect their increased musical understanding by developing their own interpretations and sense of personal style.

In order to be able to do this students will inevitably play more difficult pieces as they develop vocal and instrumental techniques, but it is through their interaction musically with each other and the audience, as well as their growing sense of musical style when performing, that their musical understanding is clearly demonstrated, and not through technical accomplishment alone.

In the early stages of composition, students can develop musical ideas within given musical structures. As they become more aware of how music reflects time, place and culture and the processes and conventions of particular styles, genres and traditions, students begin to develop compositions which are convincing in the style or for a particular occasion and purpose. More advanced composers begin to develop their own style and compose extended pieces with developed musical ideas.

Students' listening skills are demonstrated as they make connections between the music of others and the music that they create. They progress from being able to identify and describe musical features to understanding how these reflect the context of the music they are listening to.

When reviewing and evaluating, at level 4, students suggest improvements to their own and others' work. More advanced skills enable them to make improvements to their own and others' work in light of the chosen style. Furthermore, they develop and support their opinions about their work, evaluating the success of the piece in relation to the original intentions.

It is important that teachers plan activities which enable students to demonstrate their understanding at the highest level. For example, in developing performing tasks, it is vital that students have a variety of performing experiences, that they are given opportunities to take on different roles when performing and to make creative decisions when rehearsing and refining performances. If students are to develop convincing compositions with advanced understanding of musical style, we need to provide opportunities for them to make creative decisions and work more independently. When developing listening, reviewing and evaluating activities, we must encourage students to see the connections between their music and the work of others, as well as providing opportunities to justify their decisions made during the creative process.

Effective transition between Key Stage 2 and 3

Ofsted's report *Making More of Music* (2009) suggests that continuity between the primary and secondary phases in music is often 'virtually non-existent' and that the information passed from primary to secondary is often limited to which students are receiving instrumental lessons. Many students have been involved in the Wider Opportunities and Sing Up programmes during Key Stage 2, and through these and further curriculum experiences at primary level will have started to make significant progress with the Key Processes. We believe that students come to us in Year 7 with a wealth of musical experiences from musical activities both inside and outside of school and that these need to be celebrated and built upon in order to maximise progress with the Key Processes in music.

A number of schools we have worked with have developed a range of strategies for increasing the partnership between secondary and their feeder primaries. These include: liaison meetings between staff focusing on the curriculum in both schools, sharing examples of students work and secondary teachers leading music lessons in the primary school.

One approach is to develop a transition unit for the start of Year 7 to enable teachers to gain an understanding of what students can do. This should involve from the outset the integrated processes of performing, composing, listening, reviewing and evaluating. They should inspire and motivate students by challenging them with creative activities in which they can all achieve success regardless of their previous experience. This enables teachers to identify the students' understanding of the Key Processes and to start to plan for progression. A number of local authorities encourage their music teachers to use the same transition unit at the start of Year 7, so that outcomes can be shared and their judgements of students' progress can be moderated across schools.

Other initiatives include 'playing days' where secondary school ensembles work with primary students, as well as projects with visiting musicians where secondary and primary students have worked together. These activities enhance the curriculum and help both students and staff gain a greater understanding of music in the different phases. Students and staff can also get to know each other before transition takes place. Not only do these joint activities aid Year 6 to 7 transition but they can have a significant impact on the musical understanding of the secondary students involved.

In the following case study, in order to increase opportunities for students to take part in performances in different contexts and develop musical leadership skills, a Year 9 group worked with students from a feeder primary school.

The initial task was for the Year 9 students to help the primary students to present a concert. A group of secondary students were attached to each class in the primary school and worked closely with the students to help them to rehearse and perform their pieces. The concert was organised and stage managed by the secondary students. They decided the running order, word processed and printed the programme, organised publicity and front of house, and set the stage in between each performance, as well as playing with the primary students when appropriate.

At the same time back at school, the Year 9 students worked on their own performance pieces using steel pans. The lessons focused on enhancing their performing skills on steel pans and developing their arranging skills. Supported by teachers, the students chose the pieces and arranged them appropriately for the steel pan ensemble. The students performed these at a concert for the primary students.

The next part of the project was for the Year 9 group to teach a Year 6 group how to play a piece on the steel pans. Each student taught their own part to a primary student and they led the ensemble, thinking about how they could further develop and refine the performance.

The project had a real impact on developing the Year 9 students' musical skills and understanding. For example they developed their understanding of chords,

(Continued)

(Continued)

harmony and arranging, as well as developing ensemble and improvisation skills. They became much more confident and accomplished performers. In terms of musical leadership, the students demonstrated patience, encouragement and teaching skills. For example, they encouraged the primary students to listen to each other and fit their part into the ensemble as a whole, they used mnemonics to help the primary students remember their rhythms, they modelled how to hold the pan beaters to create a better sound and they reminded the primary students to be quiet at times when other parts were rehearsing. This had an impact on their own ensemble and rehearsal skills.

The project also gave the teacher an opportunity to work with the primary students and observe them developing Key Processes. She was able to build on this work at the start of Year 7 with a unit of work on Caribbean music.

Summary

The Key Processes in music are inextricably linked to each other, underpinning the Key Concept of Integration of Practice. The Key Processes outline the essential skills that students need to learn in order to make progress, but it is this integration of the processes and the constant drive to develop the depth and 'quality' of the students' musical responses which leads to increased musical understanding. It is this rather than increased 'difficulty' which should dominate teachers' planning for increasing challenge across the scheme of work in music. This holistic and integrated view of the Key Processes should also lead to integrated assessments of music progress, rather than assessments of separate performing, composing and listening skills.

Reflective Questions

1. Do my units of work develop the Key Processes in a fully integrated way?
2. How can I ensure that there are a range of performing and composing activities across the scheme of work to encourage students to experiment creatively and develop unexpected outcomes?
3. Do my units of work provide increasing challenge in the Key Processes?
4. What can I do to build on the students' previous experience and progress with the Key Processes?

Further Reading 

Burnard, P. (2009) 'Progression in musical composition', in H. Coll and A. Lamont (eds), *Sound Progress*. Matlock: National Association of Music Educators.

Spruce, G. (2007) 'Listening and appraising and the ideology of aesthetic listening', in C. Philpott and G. Spruce, *Learning to Teach Music in the Secondary School*. Abingdon: RoutledgeFalmer.

References

Block, S. and Kempton, C. (2001) 'Train rhythms', in P. Hunt (ed.), *Voiceworks: A Handbook for Singing.* Oxford: Oxford University Press.

Ofsted (2009) *Making More of Music: An Evaluation of Music in Schools 2005/08*. London: Ofsted.

Qualifications and Curriculum Authority (2007) *Music: Programme of Study for Key Stage 3 and Attainment Target*. London: QCA.

Rogers, K. (2009) 'Musical progress: it depends what you mean by ...', in H. Coll and A. Lamont (eds), *Sound Progress.* Matlock: National Association of Music Educators.

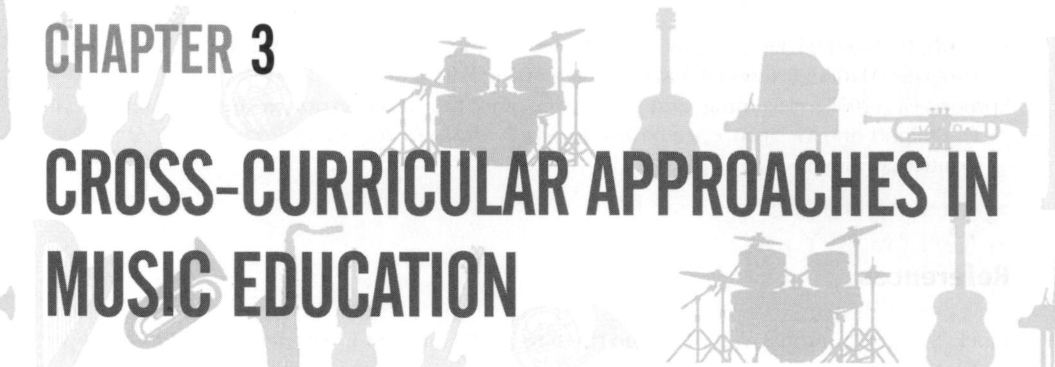

CHAPTER 3

CROSS-CURRICULAR APPROACHES IN MUSIC EDUCATION

Jonathan Savage

Introduction

The opening section of this book examined the principle curriculum frameworks that underpin teaching and learning in music. Having considered in some detail the two main frameworks of Key Concepts and Key Processes, our attention moves towards what might be considered two supporting frameworks that are implicit within the National Curriculum programme of study and related frameworks. The first of these is cross-curricularity.

What is the first thing that comes into mind when you hear the term cross-curricular? For most teachers this implies some kind of collaborative work with other colleagues. But, as we will consider below, this is only one dimension of what a cross-curricular approach to teaching music might entail. For us, a cross-curricular approach to teaching music starts with the individual teacher and their pedagogy, before extending outwards into collaborative work with others. We will investigate this approach in some detail and give examples of this approach in practice drawn from the work of one performing arts department.

Cross-curricularity in the National Curriculum

The National Curriculum contains one element that is very obviously concerned with cross-curricularity, the Cross-Curricular Dimensions. These non-statutory elements of the curriculum cover the following areas:

- Identity and cultural diversity
- Healthy lifestyles
- Community participation
- Enterprise
- Global dimensions and sustainable development
- Technology and the media
- Creativity and critical thinking.

Accompanying guidance from the QCDA (2009) outlines the purpose of these cross-curricular dimensions. They have been chosen because they reflect some of the major ideas and challenges that face us all today and will help make their learning 'real and relevant' (QCDA 2009: 1). Additionally, the dimensions:

> - are unifying areas of learning that span the curriculum and help young people make sense of the world;
> - are not subjects but are crucial aspects of learning that should permeate the curriculum and the life of a school;
> - add a richness and relevance to the curriculum experience of young people;
> - provide a focus for work within and between subjects;
> - are interdependent and mutually supportive.
>
> (QCDA 2009: 1)

At first glance, there are a number of these cross-curricular dimensions that perhaps you feel you can respond to very positively. Music education has a vital part to play in terms of community participation, creativity and critical thinking, technology and new media, for example. It would be relatively easy for many music teachers to audit their existing practice against these themes and tick many of the boxes!

However, it is important to remember that these themes are meant to inspire new cross-curricular links between subjects. In guidance material produced to accompany the cross-curricular dimensions, the following ideas were presented as possible ways forward:

- developing the dimensions through subjects, with links across subjects where there are common issues or areas of learning;
- developing the ethos of the school around a dimension;

- creating compelling learning experiences that focus on a particular dimension or combination of dimensions;
- thematic days, activity weeks or events that focus on a particular dimension being combined with lessons;
- activities being integrated into the routines of the school;
- learning outside the classroom;
- using experts from outside of the school to stimulate discussion and debate in assemblies or with specific groups of learners.

In our experiences in visiting schools to support the implementation of the new secondary curriculum we have noticed many of these things occurring. Perhaps you have taken part in collaborative, cross-curricular teaching of this type yourself? The cross-curricular dimensions certainly present an interesting set of curriculum content and ideas for staff to come together and plan, jointly, for meaningful opportunities that address the requirements of all the traditional subject areas involved.

But, helpful as these cross-curricular dimensions might be, their status as 'non-statutory' is worrying and can mean that schools, or you, could choose to ignore them! If the cross-curricular framework for music education is based on non-statutory elements, one might wonder if it is really worth considering in a book of this type. But, fortunately for our discussion and this book, there is more.

A closer look at individual subject programmes of study reveal important new emphases on collaborative, cross-subject working. In every subject's 'Curriculum Opportunities' statements you will find references such as:

- Work on problems that arise in other subjects and in contexts beyond the school (Mathematics 4d).
- Develop speaking and listening skills through work that makes cross-curricular links with other subjects (English 4f).
- Make links between science and other subjects and areas of the curriculum (Science 4k).
- Make links between geography and other subjects, including citizenship and ICT, and areas of the curriculum including sustainability and global dimension (Geography 4i).

For music, the precise statement reads:

> Make links between music and other subjects and areas of the curriculum. (QCA 2007: 184)

Perhaps you are still thinking that one sentence buried in the Curriculum Opportunities is a shallow justification for a cross-curricular approach to the teaching of music? If that is the case, read on! The strongest justification for this approach is found in the Key Concepts that should underpin all musical teaching and learning. The fourth Key Concept, 'Creativity', contains the following phrase:

> Exploring ways music can be combined with other art forms and other subject disciplines. (QCA 2007: 181)

The explanatory note that accompanies this statement is unhelpful and limiting:

> Combined with other art forms: this includes music linked to video, film, dance or drama.

Why not the visual arts? Why not some of the making practices found within the design and technology curriculum? Rather than prescribing specific cross-curricular links, the creative music teacher will want to make their own imaginative links both in terms of the curriculum content they choose to present to students and the rich cross-curricular pedagogy that they choose to skilfully develop through their classroom teaching.

But these subject references to cross-curricular opportunities are particularly helpful and represent a significant shift in the curriculum orders. They are, of course, statutory. Every teacher in every subject at Key Stage 3 is charged with developing a cross-curricular approach to teaching and learning.

Approaches to cross-curricular teaching and learning in music

For many, cross-curricular approaches to teaching and learning are about collaboration (Ofsted 2008). These collaborations may be informal, led by pairs or small groups of interested teachers. But in the majority of cases, cross-curricular work is initiated by a curriculum manager and is developed within a larger framework (e.g. a 'collapsed' timetable day, a special project of some sort, etc.). As we have seen, the National Curriculum encourages this type of collaboration and all teachers should be receptive to links being made between the areas of knowledge that are within their own and other subjects.

But we have suggested above that there is another way that cross-curricularity can be approached. This relates to the development of your own, personal pedagogy that is infused with a cross-curricular disposition. This has been defined as follows:

> A cross-curricular approach to teaching is characterised by a sensitivity towards, and a synthesis of, knowledge, skills and understandings from various subject areas. These inform an enriched pedagogy which promotes an approach to learning which embraces and explores this wider sensitivity through various methods. (Savage 2010: 8–9)

In this definition, the emphasis is placed firmly on the development of your own subject-based pedagogy. It includes a number of key ideas and terms that we will explore briefly.

Sensitivity, synthesis and subjectivity

These key words refer to the ways in which you could approach the knowledge, skills and understanding inherent within every curriculum subject. These are exemplified in curriculum documents but also have a historical legacy that is underpinned in various ways, not least in your own and others' conceptions about how each subject in the curriculum should be taught. Understanding these is a vital step that needs to be taken before considering moving into collaborative curriculum ventures or developing a cross-curricular approach within your own music teaching. As we have discussed throughout the first two chapters of this book, the Key Concepts and Key Processes that the music curriculum is built upon have a long historical legacy that is admired and respected across the world. We would not want other teachers to trample and disrespect our subject culture any more than we should disrespect theirs.

But these words also refer back to the act of teaching. In other words, they are important, informing teaching principles that impact on learning. Cross-curricular teaching is not about weakening and watering down music as a subject in any way. Rather, it is about the development of an enhanced musical pedagogy that a skilful teacher adopts for the explicit purposes of enriching teaching and learning. This leads on to the second set of key words.

Enriching, embracing and exploring

The new, enriched pedagogy of a musical, cross-curricular approach to teaching will embrace and explore your sensitivity towards, and synthesis of, the different knowledge, skills and understanding within curriculum subjects. In order for this to happen, there are at least two premises: firstly, you will need to be active in your exploration of different subjects and their associated pedagogy, embracing opportunities to make links at a content or pedagogical level as they arise; secondly, you will need to ensure that your subject knowledge is extended beyond your own subject areas. This is a challenge given the 'busyness' of everyday life as a teacher. But we would encourage you to follow your own particular interests at this point and start with what you know. There is no need to begin to make cross-curricular links with everything! Decent depth in one or two particular fields is better than broad and shallow links to everything.

Having considered some of the basic approaches towards cross-curricularity in general, we will now turn our attention to a specific example of a unit of work developed in a performing arts department whose staff were keen to develop a cross-curricular disposition and dimension in their teaching.

'Strange Fruit': a cross-curricular approach to the blues at Key Stage 3

This case study explores how a group of teachers taught the blues to students in Key Stage 3 through an imaginative application and linking together of Key Concepts in the Music, Dance and Drama curricula. The case study describes how the song 'Strange Fruit', first sung by Billie Holiday and based on a poem by Abel Meeropol, was used as a stimulus in each subject area. (See http://books.guardian.co.uk/review/story/0,,2150853,00.html for an interesting discussion of this song and its current cultural impact on the lives of some African Americans.) Please note that a film presenting the work of this case study is available for viewing at http://www.jsavage.org.uk.

Within the performing arts department at the school, Music, Drama and Dance shared an equal footing throughout Key Stage 3. At the curriculum planning level, staff identified common artistic processes and shared these with each other as key informants to their own teaching. These discussions have taken place through a planned process of In-Service Training (INSET), shared departmental meetings and workshops for staff.

For this project, one unit of work in Year 8 was considered in great detail. The Blues is a common and familiar unit of work for most music teachers. Here, this unit was taught in a way which linked together the knowledge, skills and understanding in interesting ways across the three subjects. Creativity, a Key Concept for Music in the National Curriculum, was focused on in each curriculum area. The joint approach within the unit allowed musical concepts such as syncopation, improvisation, question/answer and compositional structures to be reinforced through Dance and Drama and vice versa. Teachers mapped the creative processes involved in Music, Drama and Dance at a planning level through a curriculum audit and then used this to underpin the specific teaching in each subject area. Additionally, the strong social dimension of the blues became useful as a contextualising influence for each area of the curriculum.

The case study illustrated a number of factors relating to cross-curricular work in the performing arts. Each area of the performing arts interpreted the initial

(Continued)

(Continued)

stimulus in a variety of ways. In Drama there was a strong focus on the social/historical issues. In Music there was an initial focus on personal expression and improvisation within a pre-determined structure. But each subject was underpinned by a range of common elements that emerged, through a natural process of discussion, among staff. These elements included improvisation, syncopation and 'question and answer'. These were used to plan lessons that linked together these key elements.

Students responded very favourably to the stimulus in each area of the curriculum. They were able to make links between the subjects and recognise both the similarities and differences in elements in a subtle way, e.g. they were keen to explore improvisatory processes in music, dance and drama and relate key skills of experimentation, of trial and error and risk-taking in each subject area.

The teachers involved commented on the increasing degree of ownership that students took over their learning in the unit. The joint approach to planning resulted in a practical, activity-based curriculum that challenged students to be energised and engaged with subject content, reflective about their previous learning and actively involved in exploring the blues (e.g. through hot-seating in drama, melodic improvisation in music or through the construction of transition movements in dance).

Prior to the case study, there were significant changes to the timetable at Key Stage 3 in the performing arts faculty. These repositioned Dance on an equal footing with Music and Drama throughout in each year of Key Stage 3. As a consequence, Music lost some teaching time. However, staff commented favourably on the realignment process. If anything, the opportunities for collaborative cross-curricular work have saved all staff time. They were able to build on each other's work in new ways. All staff have noticed that the students made links in intuitive ways within and between curriculum content that was rare before.

Towards the end of this case study, the impact of this work began to extend throughout the school and beyond. Staff from the performing arts faculty led whole school INSET sessions and shared best practice teaching with colleagues from feeder primary schools. Arts practices and processes informed an innovative Personal, Social and Health Education (PSHE) curriculum entitled RESPECT. The pedagogical practices that underpinned 'Strange Fruit' began to have a much wider impact across the whole school.

Barriers to cross-curricular approaches to music education

The above case study presents a very successful example of cross-curricular practice in arts education, one in which teachers in Music, Drama and Dance worked together through planning a joint scheme of work and then delivering it, concurrently, to their classes. Perhaps this sounds a little idealistic to you, as you consider your own situation as a music teacher. There are a number of potential barriers to cross-curricular approaches which you will need to overcome in order to improve your own teaching practice in this area. These barriers are both physical and conceptual.

Physical barriers include the ways in which space is organised within the school environment. Buildings often do not facilitate cross-curricular ways of working. There are specific classes or other specialist spaces that facilitate a particular way of working. It would be hard to imagine a drama lesson in a science laboratory. This is not to say that something like this could not happen, but it would require careful thought and planning. Music classrooms are often physically isolated from other spaces (for good acoustic reasons) and this can impinge on your work. However, we would encourage every reader of this book to see what happens when you move your music teaching out of the traditional space where it occurs, perhaps into a drama studio or assembly hall. Getting rid of tables or moving away from a keyboard laboratory type space makes an enormous difference to the types of activities that a space facilitates and can challenge the ways in which we think about and organise teaching and learning in music.

Although it is not quite such an obvious physical barrier, the rigid nature of a school timetable has an impact, physically and conceptually, on approaches to cross-curricular working. The school day is divided into boxes within which subjects have to fit. Sometimes it takes a significant effort to get teachers, and pupils, to think outside these boxes and re-imagine how cross-curricular opportunities for teaching and learning could be distributed across timetabled allocations of time. However, this barrier is not insurmountable. Simple adjustments could be made to when you teach a particular unit of work. For example, I used to teach my unit of work on Gamelan music to my Year 8 classes at the same time that they were studying Islamic art in their Art and Textile lessons. This allowed me to explore the nature of patterning in the arts alongside the use of patterning within Gamelan music. Pupils would use the visual and textural patterns from their work in Art and Textiles to help develop musical patterns in their own Gamelan compositions. It saved me time in my music lessons and made an important conceptual link in their minds.

But perhaps the biggest barrier to developing a cross-curricular approach in music education is a conceptual and historical one. It is the danger of just doing things the same way that they have always been done. Ken Robinson who, in his earlier career was a Professor of the Arts at Warwick University, is one important voice who is challenging the status quo:

> Schools are obsessed with rigid timetables, for starters. If you live in a world where every lesson is 40 minutes, you immediately interrupt the flow of creativity. We need to eliminate the existing hierarchy of subjects. Elevating some disciplines over others only reinforces outmoded assumptions of industrialism and offends the principle of diversity.

> The arts, sciences, humanities, physical education, languages and maths all have equal and central contributions to make to a student's education ... The idea of separate subjects that have nothing in common offends the principle of dynamism. School systems should base their curriculum not on the idea of separate subjects, but on the much more fertile idea of disciplines ... which makes possible a fluid and dynamic curriculum that is interdisciplinary. (Robinson 2009)

While this idea is fine in theory, for many teachers today this is going to take a significant cultural and curriculum shift (and one, as we saw from our analysis of the White Paper in the foreward, is unlikely to occur over the next few years). But this does not mean to say that the point does not have value and relevance. How you imagine music education affects how you deliver music education. If your conceptual framework is tied to a model of music education that is solely about the transmission of musical knowledge, skills and processes then you may miss out on broader approaches to teaching and learning from other disciplines. As an example, let us take something as mundane as assessment. How do you assess your pupils' musical understanding? What are the common frameworks and processes that you use? Maybe you utilise techniques drawn from an 'assessment for learning' methodology, or perhaps you use the attainment target level statements from the National Curriculum. But how about the following approach drawn from the world of teaching drama?

In my drama teaching I make use of a technique called 'freeze-framing'. This is when the action in a particular scene is frozen at a particular point in time. Normally I will decide when this happens, although sometimes I will let pupils decide. At the particular moment when I shout 'Freeze!', every pupil involved in the scene has to stop what they are doing or saying and remain absolutely still. They stop moving, talking or anything else. This allows us to think together about the situation that the pupils are presenting through their acting. It is a technique drawn from the theatre and it allows a particular actor to talk about their perceptions in the situation they find themselves in or to give the audience further information about how they might be feeling or thinking. Some directors called this 'thought tracking'.

As a teacher, I use this technique quite a lot to help my understanding of whether pupils are really engaging with a particular scene. I would say it is a key part of my assessment for learning strategy. During the freeze-frame moment I will ask questions to a particular character in the scene. Sometimes I will also ask pupils who are watching the scene with me to ask questions too. I find it a very helpful way to try to understand whether or not the pupil really understands the role of their character. Obviously it has limitations. In drama, pupils often feel things that they can't express in words. But, when used with other assessment devices, freeze-framing is a really useful assessment tool. And I'm pleased that it is an adaptation of a tool from the theatre.

In this case study a drama teacher recounts her use of a particular tool, drawn from the theatre, to help assess her pupils' work. This is a specific technique that, to my knowledge, is not used in other curriculum areas. Unless you are a drama teacher, or have investigated the performance practice of the theatre in significant detail, you have probably not heard about it either. However, having found out about it here, I wonder what application you could make of it within your music teaching? What would a freeze-frame technique look or sound like in a music lesson? If you adopted it within a listening activity, what would find out about a pupil's thoughts about a piece of music? As the drama teacher mentioned in the case study, are there things in your subject that your pupils feel but might not be able to express easily in words? If so, this technique may help reveal them.

If this tool was being used in a number of different subjects, would it affect the responses that pupils make? Would they become happier with the device and respond more positively? Or would it loose its impact as it is taken outside of the context within which it has been carefully located? These are important questions that you would need to explore with the drama teacher before using the technique in your lessons. As a technique, freeze-framing may have several benefits. But there are also limitations to it, even within drama teaching (as the teacher points out in the case study). So, the tool needs to be handled carefully and with due consideration to, and sensitivity for, the context from which it has been taken. However, there may be considerable benefits in enriching one subject's assessment approach by the creative borrowing of approaches from other subjects.

Ken Robinson's call for a significant reorganisation of teaching and learning along interdisciplinary lines may be many years away. But interdisciplinary approaches to teaching and learning can be developed by teachers who are committed to broadening their pedagogies and not succumbing to the trap of just teaching one way because that this the way it has always been done. Beware of the danger of a historical pedagogical complacency. This can be a significant barrier to cross-curricular ways of thinking and working. Finally, remember that interdisciplinary work need not only be facilitated through linking the content of individual subjects in new ways. Learning more about the pedagogy that underpins different subjects is just as important and will have enriching consequences for your own subject teaching.

Summary

The call for a cross-curricular approach to teaching and learning in music is not new. Outside of formal education, the arts exist together both as distinct forms and as beautiful cross-fertilisations of ideas and practices. An analysis of any period of history will reveal how the interrelationships between art forms are central to the development of new artistic processes and products. Within education, and particularly within the arts, we have seen how a cross-curricular approach to curriculum content and pedagogy can re-inspire our approaches to music education.

Cross-curricularity provides us with an important curriculum framework that exists alongside, and within, the building blocks of a music education as presented through our analysis of Key Concepts and Key Processes in the previous two chapters. But it is important to acknowledge that curriculum subjects are, by nature and experience, very different. They have different priorities and concerns; they look, sound and speak very differently. They are underpinned by historical legacies (sometimes known as subject cultures) which affect the styles of teaching and learning that are promoted within them. These can become embodied in the pedagogies of different teachers; some may have a more traditional approach, others are more contemporary in their practice. As a teacher of music, you will have to decide how the competing approaches and pedagogies of music education will blend together within your work. You will also find it interesting to see how the pedagogies used and developed within other subject cultures can be applied and developed within your own teaching. But however you do this, a cross-curricular 'disposition' in your teaching will have many benefits for yourself and your students. This is partly because the notion of a subject 'boundary' is artificial and divisive. There is a large literature as to why the notion of 'subject' has been used as a organising tool within education. But outside the immediate educational context, as we have seen, artists, musicians, film-makers and others move between these 'boundaries' with a fluidity and ease that is difficult to replicate in our schools.

One of the very obvious benefits of cross-curricular teaching and learning in music that was exemplified by the 'Strange Fruit' case study builds on the concept of the individual subject and how it relates to other subjects within the larger organisation of the curriculum. Staff working together in the case study found that the potential of the combined subjects is greater than that of any of the individual parts. Artistic collaborations can result in a greater sense of clarity and distinctiveness in terms of the chosen artistic processes that are undertaken. The same is true for educational collaborations. But beyond that, the combinations allow for playfulness around the edges of the subjects that can bring in much more of value for teaching and learning processes then those achieved by an insular, subject-orientated approach. This playfulness within each individual teacher's pedagogy came about through their shared sense of communal enquiry in the Year 8 unit of work, through being open to the ideas and practices of other art forms, and being willing to develop and extend their own subject pedagogy in new, creative ways. This creative element can make teaching a highly enjoyable process of discovery and invention.

As arts educators we have a responsibility to encourage this playful approach to cross-curricularity because it is an intrinsic part of what we do as practising artists. How do you sum up what you do as a musician, performer or composer? Here is our attempt: we play and recreate things; we put things together, craft and build; we edit and experiment; we take things and relocate them, finding new meanings in things (sometimes in the things that may seem meaningless); we touch, feel, explore and create; we cherish the new and embellish the old, recreate and enhance, express, regress and, on occasions, digress. But surely as musicians, creativity is central to everything we do, whether it be performing, composing, listening, reviewing or evaluating. Our approach to teaching, learning and curriculum development as music educators should be as rich as our artistic endeavours in this respect. The Key Concept of creativity is central to our work. But it is not solely about the curriculum content or how it is organised; it is fundamentally about our pedagogy – who and what we are as music teachers.

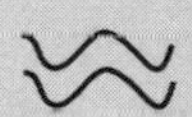

Reflective Questions

1. What are the elements within my own subject pedagogy that make it difficult to work in a cross-curricular way? How could I begin to mitigate the effects of these?
2. What does a cross-curricular 'disposition' in music teaching really look like? If it is about my individual pedagogy, how can I begin to analyse that and develop cross-curricular links in my own work at this fundamental level?
3. To what extent can I strengthen the collaborative elements of cross-curricularity within my teaching? What strategies of professional or curriculum development could I employ to do this? Are there like-minded staff that I could work with in developing these ideas in my school?
4. How can I broaden my knowledge of other subject areas, including their subject pedagogies, to ensure that I treat them with the respect and dignity that they deserve?

Further Reading

Fautley, M. and Savage, J. (2010) *Cross-curricular Teaching and Learning in the Secondary School: The Arts*. London: Routledge.

Savage, J. (2010) *Cross-curricular Teaching and Learning in the Secondary School*. London: Routledge.

'Strange Fruit' case study video. Online at: http://www.jsavage.org.uk (accessed 20 November 2010).

Further case studies exploring cross-curricularity in music education can be found at: http://www.name.org.uk/projects/ks3/case-studies.

References

Ofsted (2008) *Curriculum Innovation in Schools*. London: Ofsted.

Qualifications and Curriculum Authority (2007) *Music: Programme of Study for Key Stage 3 and Attainment Target*. London: QCA.

Qualifications and Curriculum Development Agency (2009) *Cross-curriculum Dimensions: A Planning Guide for Schools*. London: QCDA. Also available from: http://curriculum.qcda.gov.uk/key-stages-3-and-4/cross-curriculum-dimensions/index.aspx (accessed 12 February 2010).

Robinson, K. (2009) 'Fertile minds need feeding', *Guardian*, 10 February. Online at: http://www.guardian.co.uk/education/2009/feb/10/teaching-sats (last accessed 15 December 2010).

Savage, J. (2010) *Cross-curricular Teaching and Learning in the Secondary School*. London: Routledge.

CHAPTER 4

PERSONAL, LEARNING AND THINKING SKILLS AND FUNCTIONAL SKILLS

Carolyn Cooke

Introduction

The National Curriculum's aims are to 'enable all young people to become successful learners, confident individuals and responsible citizens' (QCDA 2007b). These aims are achieved through a combination of learning in individual subjects and, as we have outlined in the last chapter, engaging students in cross-curricular learning. The National Curriculum acknowledges that students also need to develop a range of transferable learning skills. Personal Learning and Thinking Skills (PLTS), alongside Functional Skills, provide the framework for planning, teaching and making students' aware of these transferable skills within individual subjects, as well as within whole-school contexts.

It is generally considered that music teaching develops more than just musical understanding and musicianship. This is highlighted in the Importance Statement which states:

> Music brings together intellect and feeling and enables personal expression, reflection and emotional development as well as recognising that positive interaction with music can develop pupils' competence as learners. (QCA 2007b: 179)

Therefore, music seems well placed to contribute to the development of PLTS and Functional Skills. However, as suggested earlier, defining music education solely by its ability to contribute to broader curriculum aims is to lose sight of its own unique contribution to students' learning. Therefore, in this chapter we will argue that the thoughtful integration of PLTS and Functional Skills into relevant, authentic musical experiences can help ensure that the curriculum provides rich musical learning for all students.

The questions this chapter will address are:

- What teaching and learning strategies can support and promote PLTS and Functional Skills within musical contexts?
- How can we engage students in understanding their own learning in and beyond the music classroom?

PLTS and Functional Skills

There are six Personal Learning and Thinking Skills (PLTS) that students should be developing across the KS3 curriculum (see Table 4.1).

Functional Skills consist of three skills areas: ICT, English and Mathematics. The performance statements for each of the areas can be seen in Table 4.2.

Table 4.1 PLTS and its focus

PLTS	Pupils
Independent enquirers	• Process and evaluate information in their investigations • Plan what to do and how to go about it. • Take informed and well-reasoned decisions • Recognise that others have different beliefs and attitudes
Reflective learners	• Evaluate their strengths and limitations • Set themselves realistic goals with criteria for success • Monitor their own performance and progress • Invite feedback from others • Make changes to further their learning
Effective participants	• Actively engage with issues that affect them and those around them • Play a full part in the life of their school, college, workplace or wider community • Take responsible action to bring improvements for others as well as themselves
Team workers	• Work confidently with others, adapting to different contexts and taking responsibility for their own part • Listen to and take account of different views
Creative thinkers	• Form collaborative relationships, resolving issues to reach agreed outcomes • Generate and explore ideas and make original connections • Try different ways to tackle a problem • Work with others to find imaginative solutions and outcomes that are of value
Self-managers	• Organise themselves, showing personal responsibility, initiative, creativity and enterprise • Are committed to learning and self-improvement • Actively embrace change, responding positively to new priorities, coping with challenges and looking for opportunities

Adapted from QCDA (2007a).

Table 4.2 Functional Skills and their performance statements

English	Mathematics	ICT
Speaking, listening and communication	Representing – selecting the mathematics and information required to model a situation	Using ICT
Reading	Analysing – processing and using mathematics	Finding and selecting information
Writing	Interpreting and communicating the results of the analysis	Developing, presenting and communicating information

Source: DCSF (2010).

Both PLTS and Functional Skills provide a framework to help students understand their own learning and how these skills can transfer between different contexts. Transfer of learning might be between different subjects, for example a student develops their ability to ask other students for feedback on their work in English which they then utilise during music lessons to help improve their performance or composition. Transfer of knowledge and understanding between different musical contexts is also integral as can be seen in the Key Concepts of Critical Understanding 'Draw on experience of a wide range of musical contexts and styles to inform judgements' and Creativity 'Using existing musical knowledge, skills and understanding for new purposes and in new contexts' (QCA 2007b). Equally, students could transfer learning that has been developed in extra-curricular music activities, instrumental or vocal lessons, or community music groups, which often get left outside the classroom door.

Integration of PLTS and Functional Skills into meaningful musical experiences not only maintains the unique nature of the subject, but also makes engagement with the skills more sustainable, rather than students sensing it as just a bit tagged on to lessons in order to meet a target. Ensuring the skills are fully integrated and opportunities are provided to develop them requires careful planning and choosing appropriate teaching and learning strategies. The next section will explore how this can be achieved within the music curriculum by considering PLTS and Functional Skills at three levels:

- when shaping the curriculum across Key Stage 3;
- when designing or reviewing units of work;
- when planning individual lessons.

Planning for PLTS and Functional Skills across KS3

The broad range of musical styles, genres and traditions that students experience during Key Stage 3 each have specific qualities that can be used to develop PLTS and Functional Skills within the musical contexts. It is through the careful selection and arrangement of units of work to cover a broad range of musical contexts that students' learning, thinking and functional skills can all be developed as an integral part of their musical learning. Examples of how different units of work can develop different skills and be organised to support progress in using these skills are given below.

A Year 7 unit on Samba, with its carnival context and potential for large group performance, will provide opportunities for students to develop their 'Effective Participant' and 'Team Worker' skills within a samba band. Within this large group scenario, students will assist in shaping the performance, composing sections and critiquing the effects. The teacher will use the scheme to highlight and ask students to reflect on what it means to be an effective participant and team worker in this context. This learning will then be transferred into the next unit on the blues. Students will work in smaller groups in keeping with traditional rural Blues. They will need to apply the skills for being an 'Effective Participant' and 'Team Worker' in a different way and will be asked to reflect on how they learned and made musical decisions as a group.

A Year 8 Dance Music unit, which utilises a sequencing package, allows students to select and manipulate pre-existing loops to create a dance composition in a range of styles. This provides the transferable music ICT skills to support their film compositions later in the year where they have the choice to use the ICT if they think it will help achieve the affect they want. They use the ICT in a more experimental, independent way by layering loops, recorded sounds and live performance to create their compositions.

Planning for PLTS and Functional Skills within a unit of work

As well as considering the unique nature of the musical context and how this can promote and develop certain PLTS or Functional Skills, it is also necessary to consider the type of learning experiences within each unit of work. When first looking at the six PLTS it is noticeable how integral they all seem to music and, more importantly, to what it means to be a musician. It would be hard to imagine a jazz trumpeter, a rock guitarist or a violinist who did not have highly developed skills in all these areas. Carefully planning activities that are musical (where students are responding to or participating in music) is therefore key in delivering PLTS through the Music curriculum.

Having thought about the musical contexts of the units, it is helpful to consider how progress in PLTS and Functional Skills can be supported. Progression in Functional Skills is described as being 'determined by students applying skills with increasing independence to more complex and less familiar situations' (DCSF 2010), while the guidance on PLTS in Music suggests it might be seen as learners demonstrating that they are:

- making personal choices about their learning and identifying ways to improve their work;
- drawing on their own experiences and making connections with different musical activities and with other areas of the arts;
- extending and transferring their skills and understanding with more confidence and creativity;
- engaging with and applying their music beyond school contexts for a specific purpose.

(QCDA 2007c)

Essentially, what both these definitions are describing are students who are capable of independent learning, but how can we plan a scheme of work that gradually builds to this? Table 4.3 shows a possible model that could be used to design opportunities to develop students' independence across the Key Stage.

Of course, there is a time and place for all three types of learning depending on the class, unit of work or year group, but Table 4.3 demonstrates one

Table 4.3 A possible transition towards Independent Learning

	Structured Learning	Guided Learning	Independent Learning
Teacher	Teacher-led – provides knowledge and closely directs the learning.	Provides a framework of knowledge and resources and scaffolds the learning to enable pupils to reach their potential.	Facilitates the pupils to direct their own learning.
Objectives and outcomes	Demonstrates the objectives and outcomes through completing planned tasks and activities to replicate the teacher's expectations.	Demonstrates the objectives and outcomes by using the teacher's modelling and scaffolding to shape the tasks and activities in their own way.	Approaches the objectives in different ways. Will often lead to unexpected musical outcomes.
Pupils	Follow the directions of the teacher as closely as possible.	Use the scaffolding and modelling of the teacher as a basis for their own learning and experimenting.	Approaches teacher for help and advice. Uses the teacher's expertise and knowledge of resources as well as drawing on other pupils' expertise.
Creativity	Replication of teacher model.	Redefining the teacher's model to include their own ideas and solutions.	Redirection, reconstruction or integration of ideas to create own model.
PLTS and Functional Skills	Pupils experience and are taught what PLTS and Functional Skills mean in musical contexts through carefully planned activities and tasks.	Pupils transfer PLTS and Functional Skills to new contexts understanding how they need to be adapted and beginning to use them more autonomously.	Pupils draw on and apply the full range of PLTS and Functional Skills to enable them to achieve the musical outcomes they want without being led.

model for judging whether there are sufficient opportunities and potential for students to develop PLTS and functional skills. Some students may be able to work in a more independent way on certain types of tasks from an early stage while others may struggle even towards the end of the Key Stage. Personalisation of the learning is essential, as is developing a number of teaching strategies that will enable this type of independent learning to take place.

Below are some examples of such teaching and learning strategies. The first example demonstrates how a structured musical experience can introduce students to a specific PLTS. The second example is a mystery activity (based on Leading in Learning materials DfES 2005) which develops a range of PLTS and Functional Skills and the third outlines a Year 9 project which promotes independent, student-led learning.

Developing reflective learners

At the start of Year 7, while learning about Djembe drumming, students are guided through a series of experiences over three lessons to understand what it means to be reflective learners in music.

- *Lesson 1*. Students create a whole-class performance of a Djembe piece. Some students lead sections so that the teacher is a learner as well. She models the skills by reflecting on her own performance and ability to learn.
- *Lesson 2*. Students watch a video clip of a previous student group performing a Djembe composition and identify what made it effective as a Djembe piece. They then design success criteria for their own class performance. Students revisit the whole-class performance and make improvements. The performance is recorded and the students are asked to reflect on the outcome in relation to the success criteria.
- *Lesson 3*. Students compose a Djembe piece in groups. After five minutes the teacher indicates to the groups that there are some questions on the board. The questions include 'What is working well?' 'How can we improve what we are doing?' 'What have we tried that hasn't worked?' After ten minutes she reminds the groups again of the questions. Afterwards she asks them to discuss what impact the questions had on what they did. She also asks them to think individually about what they had learned over the three lessons, how they learned it and if they found learning in this way easy or difficult.

This sequence of lessons develops students' ability to:

- reflect critically on their own and others work (*reflective learner*);
- establish their own success criteria based on knowledge of the musical tradition (*reflective learner*);

- engage with feedback from the teacher and peers (*reflective learner*);
- independently monitor and improve their learning (*self-manager*);
- actively engage with the task and their peers to achieve at their best (*effective participant*);
- make group decisions about the direction of the task (*team worker*);
- find musical solutions to issues (*creative thinker*).

Mystery activities to develop PLTS and Functional Skills

Year 8 students are at the start of a unit on programme music. The students have listened to, discussed and tried playing some extracts from Benjamin Britten's *Four Sea Interludes* from *Peter Grimes*. The teacher now wants them to create their own musical ideas for a composition about the sea.

At the start of the lesson the teacher displays a picture of a boat leaving a harbour in calm waters. He asks the students to discuss the musical effect they would want to create to represent the picture and then experiment with different musical ideas. After ten minutes he 'conducts' the groups by bringing them in and fading them out until the class has heard a section of ideas from each group. They then briefly discuss the atmosphere that has been created and the similarities and differences in the way the task was approached.

At this point he brings up three newspaper headlines: 'Severe storm warning – sailors advised to stay at home', 'Beautiful summer's day ahead. Record crowds expected' and 'Boatman named as a hero after saving boy from cliff fall'. He gives the students ten minutes to choose a headline, modify their initial ideas to reflect the new information and compose some ideas for an ending. After ten minutes each group performs and the class is asked to guess which headline they chose and why. Each performing group is then asked to explain what they modified and why, as well as justifying their musical decisions.

This lesson is developing students' ability to:

- process and evaluate information in order to take well-reasoned decisions (*independent enquirer*);
- make changes and improvements to their own work based on understanding the nature of the task (*reflective learner*);
- cope with unexpected changes (*self-manager*);
- work effectively within a group to come to collective decisions (*team worker*);
- come up with musical solutions to new situations (*creative thinker*);
- explaining and justifying their choices (*English functional skills*).

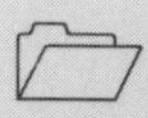

A Year 9 student-led learning experience

Students have learned about a variety of styles, genres and traditions during Key Stage 3 including Indian Classical Music, Calypso, Dance Music and African Drumming. During the spring term of Year 9, students are given the opportunity to draw on all their musical learning and skills in a scheme of work on Fusion. The role of the teacher in this unit is to facilitate the students' own exploration of this topic and therefore the first lesson starts with the students getting into groups and deciding what they want to achieve from the project. The students set their own learning objectives and questions to answer. Each group researches the two traditions they intend to 'fuse' and spend time collecting resources, which includes making decisions about whether and how to use ICT and listening to examples of fusion. The students draw on their own musical and learning skills and those of others within the group to plan and carry out the project, asking the teacher to model or suggest ways of using the resources if they need to.

At the end of each lesson the students use an online blog to record what was achieved in the lesson, what decisions were made and justifying why, and what their individual contribution was. They were also encouraged to write about their learning; was it effective? could it have been done in a different way?

This scheme develops students' ability to:

- transfer knowledge and skills between different contexts adapting them to make appropriate musical decisions (*creative thinker*);
- reflect on what it means to succeed in a longer-term project (*reflective learner*);
- draw on their own and other people's abilities to achieve the goal (*independent enquirer*);
- decide what to learn and how best to learn it by drawing on appropriate resources (*independent enquirer, self-manager*);
- draw on a range of ICT to support their learning, both of the musical traditions being used and to support their music-making (*ICT functional skills*);
- discuss and listen to each other's ideas and write a personal learning account of the project (*English functional skills*).

Two common themes emerge from these examples: meta-learning and students' ownership of their learning. Both these themes will be discussed in the next section.

PLTS and Functional Skills in individual lessons: meta-learning and ownership

In his book *Classrooms as Learning Communities*, Watkins talks of meta-cognition being defined as 'thinking about thinking' and coins the phrase meta-learning to describe 'learning about learning' (Watkins 2005). He argues that meta-learning is crucial in developing students' ability to transfer skills between different learning contexts.

By making the learning process involved in musical activities explicit, and by using the language of PLTS and Functional Skills in individual lessons to provide students with a way of communicating their ideas and feelings on learning, students will begin to develop their meta-learning skills.

Watkins suggests four ways that this can be achieved, all of which appear within the examples in the previous section:

- ***Making learning an object of attention***. Students in the first example were asked to reflect on what it was they had learned and whether it was easy or difficult learning in this way, while the students in the third example were asked to reflect on how they had chosen to learn and whether there were alternatives.
- ***Making learning an object of conversation***. Students in all three examples were asked to discuss their contribution and the processes they had gone through.
- ***Making learning an object of reflection***. Students in example three used an online blog to enable them to see the wider picture of their learning over the course of a project.
- ***Making learning an object of learning***. Students in all three examples were made aware of the skills they were developing and each example demonstrated a higher level of individual control (ownership) over the learning process than the previous one.

Some schools have decided that all lessons should have a learning objective to address PLTS or Functional Skills alongside the subject objectives with the aim of making the learning of these skills explicit. If the integration of skills within the musical experience is key to ensuring their relevance and sustainability, adding a learning objective such as 'Understand how to participate effectively in a rock band' seems to take us back to a tokenistic approach we are trying to avoid. As well as putting emphasis onto the skill rather than the musical learning or effect of being an effective participant in this context, it also ignores the fact that some students might learn skills as a reflective learner, a creative thinker or a self-manager from the same task. A student's musical learning is by its nature individual. Therefore, a sense of students owning and shaping the learning, rather than the learning 'being done to them', is important in developing their own understanding of their learning. Spruce (2009) describes a student who 'has ownership of what and how they learn' as an 'empowered learner'. He argues that it is through this empowerment that 'critical thinking and understanding can be developed or demonstrated', something that is equally important in developing students' knowledge of their own learning as it is for developing their musical knowledge. Some strategies and examples for empowering learners in music lessons are outlined below with the common thread that they all involve students in discussing the learning process therefore developing their 'meta-learning' skills:

- Giving students ownership of ***what*** they learn. For example, at the start of a new unit of work the students watch and listen to a few examples of the chosen style, genre or tradition. Each student is then asked to suggest two questions they want to explore by the end of the unit (one about the context of the music and one about the music itself). These are put on a wall display and returned to at various points in the unit to be answered, modified or added to.
- Giving students ownership of ***how*** they learn. Providing students with the opportunity and confidence to say 'I would learn that best by ...' This might involve working alone rather than in a group, using notation rather than graphic score or using an instrument they are learning rather than those in the classroom.
- Giving students ownership of their ***assessment***. Encouraging students to ask for formative feedback from peers and teachers when they feel it is appropriate, rather than waiting for an organised plenary session. Assessment for Learning then becomes student controlled and more meaningful in providing feedback which can have a direct impact on work during the lesson rather than at the end where ideas cannot then be experimented with.

Meta-learning and ownership in a film music project

A group of students want to build tension into their film composition. They have identified three musical elements they want to analyse for their impact on the atmosphere: texture, pitch and rhythm. They have decided as a group to make a graphic score of a clip from the film *Titanic* they have chosen to analyse. They have a timeline across the bottom and then each takes an element and graphically notates the music. They then compare each other's scores and use these as a basis for their own composition. During the composition process they frequently revisit the scores if they feel they are not creating the effect they want in order to help evaluate what they need to do to improve.

(Continued)

(Continued)

This lesson develops students' ability to:

- process and evaluate information (*independent enquirer*);
- reflect on the musical outcomes and ask for feedback (*reflective learner*);
- plan their own learning (*self-manager*);
- organise and manage their roles within the group (*effective participant*);
- find creative solutions to a compositional problem (*creative thinker*);
- represent information, analyse information and apply it (*Maths functional skills*).

Summary

Many schools have adopted initiatives to help students become better learners. Whether it is Social and Emotional Aspects of Learning (SEAL), Learning to Learn, Arts Awards, Open Minds or Building Learning Power, there is a common understanding that students need to develop more than just subject knowledge to be successful in education and life. The inclusion of PLTS and Functional Skills at the centre of the curriculum experience is therefore an important statement of intent, that learning these skills is not just the domain of PSHE or pastoral lessons but should be at the centre of all learning in every subject.

This chapter has outlined how developing PLTS and Functional Skills brings together a number of significant strands in current educational thinking about learning: independent learning, personalisation, higher-order thinking skills such as meta-cognition and meta-learning, and ownership of learning. Through the examples and strategies we have also outlined how the different musical contexts of units of work can be utilised to develop these skills through meaningful musical activities and how developing these skills across the Key Stage requires a shift in the role of the teacher, from provider of knowledge, resources and activities to facilitator of independent learning. It is through designing the learning in this way that developing PLTS and Functional Skills through music will impact on students' engagement with the subject, the developmental progress they make and, most importantly of all, their musicianship.

Reflective Questions

1. Is there progression in my units of work towards open-ended tasks and activities that allow students to experiment creatively, taking their learning in unexpected directions?

(Continued)

(Continued)

2. How can I empower students to have a voice in deciding what they learn and how they learn it?
3. How can I encourage students to ask for feedback and discuss their learning with each other during lessons rather than only in teacher-led plenary sessions?
4. How can I develop plenary feedback sessions to provide more meaningful discussions about learning and learning processes and the impact these have on the musical outcomes? What are the alternatives to 'one positive comment and one area for development' in supporting students thinking about learning in music?
5. What can I do to reinforce, extend and transfer learning that happens in musical activities beyond the classroom (e.g. between extra-curricular activities, peripatetic teaching, community music groups, student-led musical activities)?

Further Reading

Musical Futures (2006) *Teacher's Resources Section 1: Personalising Music Learning*. Online at: http://www.musicalfutures.org/resource/27234 (accessed 15 August 2010).

Philpott, C. (2007) 'Musical learning and musical development', in C. Philpott and G. Spruce, *Learning to Teach Music in the Secondary School: A Companion to School Experience*. London: Routledge.

Philpott, C. (2009) 'Personalising learning in music education', in J. Evans and C. Philpott, *A Practical Guide to Teaching Music in the Secondary School.* London: Routledge.

References

DCSF (2010) *Functional Skills Support Programme: Developing Functional Skills in Music*. Online at: http://nationalstrategies.standards.dcsf.gov.uk/node/312119?uc=force_uj (accessed 15 August 2010).

DfES (2005) *Leading in Learning: Exemplification in Music*. Online at: http://nationalstrategies.standards.dcsf.gov.uk/node/95746 (accessed 15 August 2010).

Qualifications and Curriculum Authority (2007) *Music: Programme of Study for Key Stage 3 and Attainment Target*. London: QCA.

Qualifications and Curriculum Development Agency (2007a) *Skills (PLTS and Functional Skills)*. Online at: http://curriculum.qcda.gov.uk/key-stages-3-and-4/skills/index.aspx (accessed 15 August 2010).

Qualifications and Curriculum Development Agency (2007b) *PLTS in Music*. Online at: http://curriculum.qcda.gov.uk/key-stages-3-and-4/subjects/key-stage-3/music/PLTS-in-Music/index.aspx (accessed 15 August 2010).

Spruce, G. (2009) 'Teaching and Learning for Critical Thinking and Understanding', in J. Evans and C. Philpott, *A Practical Guide to Teaching Music in the Secondary School.* London: Routledge.

Watkins, C. (2005) *Classrooms as Learning Communities: What's in It for Schools?* London: Routledge.

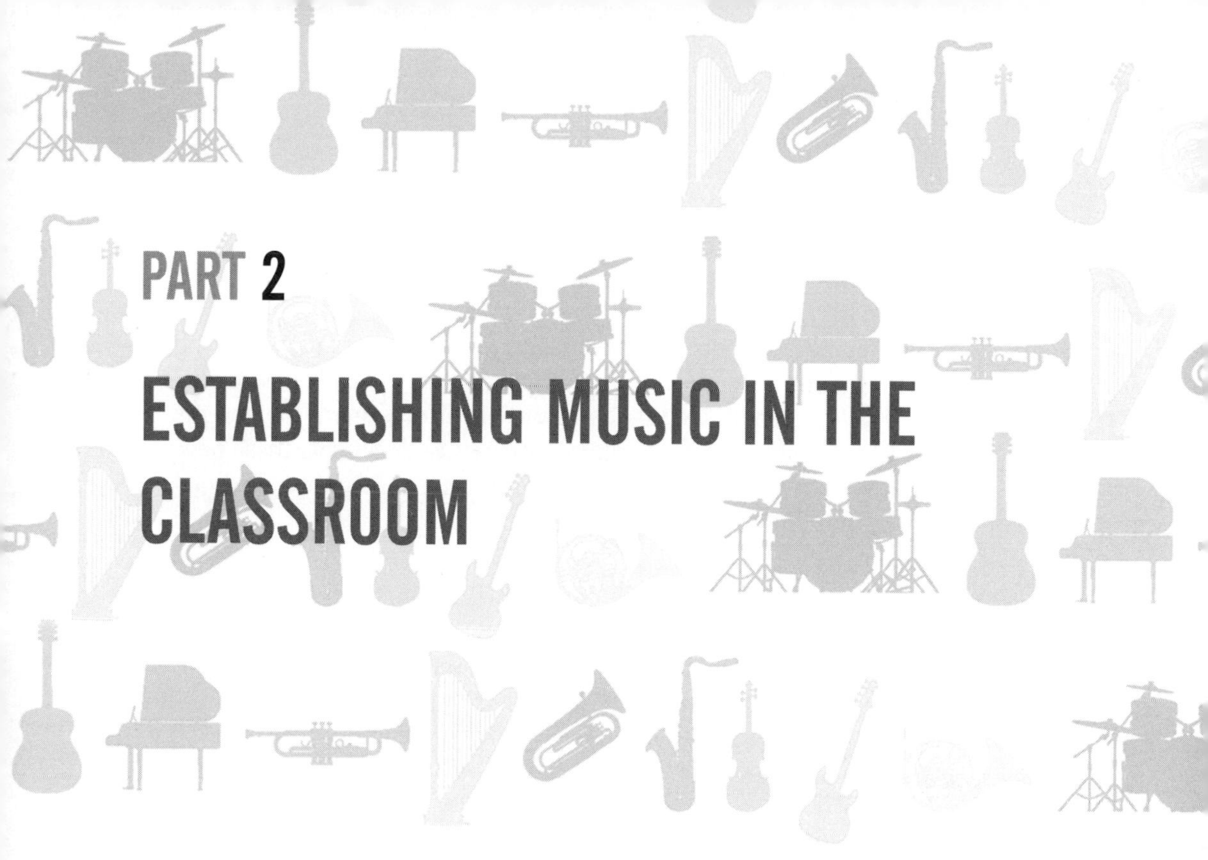

PART 2

ESTABLISHING MUSIC IN THE CLASSROOM

This section looks in greater detail at the Range and Content and the Curriculum Opportunities sections of the secondary curriculum for music, particularly focusing on those aspects which are new. The aim here is to explore how these aspects might be approached in practice. These chapters will outline examples and case studies and also recommend resources which are useful in helping teachers to implement these aspects of the curriculum.

CHAPTER 5

DEVELOPING PERFORMING OPPORTUNITIES

Anthony Anderson

Introduction

Having outlined the key curriculum frameworks that underpin the music curriculum in the first section of this book, we now turn our attention to the Range and Content and the Curriculum Opportunities sections of the National Curriculum. These aspects outline the breadth of musical experiences we should draw on and the opportunities we should provide to enhance students' learning and engagement with the Key Concepts and Key Processes.

As we have emphasised throughout this book, music education is for everyone, offering something unique to students from all backgrounds and cultures. It is a powerful medium for developing creativity and expression. It enables students of all abilities to achieve and to build confidence and self-esteem. These are the kinds of statements that motivate us as music educators to deliver the accessible and engaging music education to which young people are entitled.

However, if we are honest, it does not always work out quite like this in practice, especially in the area of musical performance. The truth is that it is all too easy to present opportunities only to the more able. When founding an ensemble for a school performance, looking for students to showcase the best work during a head teacher's lesson observation or demonstrating the strengths of the music department during an open day, our mission statement that music is for all can often be conveniently placed to one side. We gather the most able, the most reliable and the easiest students to manage and trust that they will rise to the occasion, and they usually do.

While this is understandable to a certain extent, there is a better way than this. This chapter will consider ideas and examples of how to provide *all* students with performance opportunities both in and outside of the classroom. This is vitally important if, as teachers, we are to provide the best possible opportunities for all students. Celebrating and encouraging student achievement at all levels and enabling performance needs to be a key strand in all our musical teaching and learning.

Musical performance at the heart of the curriculum

Performing for all is a key element in the music curriculum and a primary skill for developing successful learners, confident individuals and responsible citizens as students become active musicians. As students are engaged in producing musical performances in a range of different styles, they begin to understand musical traditions, explore music in context and appreciate unfamiliar music.

The Range and Content section of the National Curriculum requires teachers to provide performing activities in a range of contexts, both within and beyond the classroom, for all students. This is not as impossible as it might at first appear, and the curriculum orders themselves suggest student concerts, public concerts, assemblies, rehearsals, formal and informal external events and online performance events. These present a good starting point and, in this chapter, we will present a range of ideas and examples which music teachers will be able to develop for their own learning context. This is an important attitude and approach in this revision of the curriculum and, as always, schemes of work and lesson content must be adapted to best suit year groups, classes and individuals.

In thinking about what such principles might look like in practice, it is necessary to look at performance both within and outside the classroom. What are the principles and approaches that are most helpful in considering how to deliver a high-quality approach to music performance?

Performance opportunities inside the classroom

Performing as a vehicle for learning

Performing should be a fundamental element within all classroom teaching. Performing is the most effective means of learning and experiencing music. It enables students to go on their own learning journey of discovery because, as John Paynter said, 'without a sense of adventure, true education is impossible' (Paynter 1970, cited in Mills and Paynter 2008). Starter tasks can be a particularly good place from which to begin this approach. As an example, at the start of a lesson on minimalism, rather than explaining the concept of a minimalist cell, then asking students to write their own, a possible alternative would be to ask student pairs to use only the black notes of the keyboard (pentatonic) to write a five-note melody. This short two-minute task can be followed by a class performance as the teacher facilitates each pair to enter and build the texture, each repeating their idea until everyone in the group is playing (including the teacher). From this, the teacher can ask the students to draw out the features of minimalism and then introduce lesson objectives arising from this opening task.

Planning for musical performance

Enabling all to participate in class performance takes planning and behind-the-scenes preparation. Performance elements will need to be differentiated to enable everyone to participate on an equal footing and there needs to be appropriate stretch and challenge for all. It is just as tragic for those who can play a musical instrument never to have the opportunity to use this as part of a curriculum music lesson as it is for those who have never had this chance not to be empowered to fully participate. More able musicians must be challenged and not just asked to repeat or do more of the same task. In preparing a lesson, you should consider how all can be enabled to make the most of performance opportunities, be ready to demonstrate what this means for their learning and ensure the performance task is relevant to the particular topic area. This will not happen by default and must be planned for in a deliberate manner. It may make considerable additional demands on the teacher, but the rewards of a fully integrated performance enabling engaged musical learning are surely worth the blood, sweat and tears!

Why not consider developing performance settings in which talented music students become the lynchpin that holds the performance together? Music can be arranged to enable this, but sometimes personal directions from the teacher can be more effective. Expect these students to add something special and to take responsibility for the quality of music-making within a group. Allow them opportunities to direct and shape performances through conducting skills. This need not mean a waving of arms, but can also take place from an instrument, with the student leading others in a truly engaging and fresh musical experience. This should be enough to challenge any musician, including the teacher!

At one school, the teacher wanted to involve all students in understanding what it was like to play the piano, not just those who had some ability in this area. The answer was to arrange a Chopin prelude into eight different differentiated parts with a variety of notation systems. This led to a class performance on keyboards in which all were involved and all enabled to understand something of this style of performance.

Leading from the front

Always be ready to demonstrate and challenge learning through modelling musical performance rather than solely relying on verbal instruction. This consistently develops understanding and enables students to reflect constructively on their own performing and make comparisons between their own and your musical performance. Developing this 'teacher performer' identity should be built upon your own, hopefully ongoing, musical experiences. It is a central plank in learning to teach music musically.

Teachers can facilitate musical leadership in students by not restricting their ideas, even when they do not fall within the set brief. It is much better to work with emerging ideas and to see what can be accomplished with them rather than crushing initial enthusiasm with a 'No, that's not what we are doing today' response. Teachers play a crucial role in using their musical skills and experience to evaluate the roles taken up within a musical ensemble and by encouraging leadership in its various forms, while challenging the whole group.

Using technology to help 'personalise' performance opportunities

The recording of student work should be an integral part of each lesson. Opportunities for students to reflect on their own performances and have access to a library of their own digital recordings at all times will strengthen their musical development and allow for greater continuity between lessons. In a similar manner, as we will see in Chapter 7, music technology can be dovetailed into class performances with the use of DJ'ing, sequencing programs such as Logic, Garageband or Cubase, and other devices. Mobile phones, iPod touch and other devices which students bring with them to lessons can be a useful way to supplement the available music technology. The use of such technology can be an aid to performance for those students who have untapped skills in these areas, enabling all to be fully involved in performance.

Valuing the technology that students bring with them to a lesson was given an interesting twist in one school where, an 'iJam' was developed. Rather than students being asked to put their iPods away, they were asked to get them out of their bags and make music together. This involved downloading suitable apps, linking iPods to a suitable PA system and developing performance and composition tasks, with different students working with the teacher to develop their parts.

Integration of practice

Finally in this section on approaches to high-quality musical performance within the classroom, the sequence of learning in a lesson needs to be carefully structured so that performing, composing and listening tasks are integrated together and develop naturally. For example, listening tasks need to have a focus and could lead towards performance work, which could then include group composition and an opportunity for students to develop their own ideas. As part of this process, performance tasks need to be given proper space and time so that they can be understood by the students as having real value. Providing enough time for students to originate and refine ideas and to perform them in the context of their class is vital if the validity of the task is to be reinforced. Integrated peer assessment of these performances can act as a springboard to musical development and will be a crucial part of this. A head pat from the teacher that performances are all 'very good' will not fool savvy young people. Proper evaluation including strengths and areas for development in which peers, group members and the teacher all have an input will help the task to be valued. It must not only be the most able groups or the most polished performances that are aired. All need and deserve the opportunity to trial their ideas in the classroom arena.

Performance opportunities outside the classroom

Providing performance opportunities for all outside the classroom can be more of a challenge, especially with limited funding and the logistics of organising teachers and resources. However, there are no limits on creativity or imaginative solutions! With a little thought and some careful reflection it is possible to create more opportunities for students to perform outside of the classroom than the initial panic at this thought might suggest. The following principles and approaches start with ideas related to developing performance within the school, then extending approaches between 'networks' of schools before, finally, considering broader and more extensive partnerships that teachers may want to develop.

Removing the walls from your music department

As we considered in Chapter 3, a cross-curricular approach to teaching and learning in music can facilitate a range of opportunities for music performance outside your classroom. Combining classes to work on a joint drama and music project can be a simple but effective idea which could result in performances to peers or other year groups. Spreading the net wider may provide even more enriching experiences with other areas of learning. The cross-curriculum dimensions of identity and cultural diversity, healthy lifestyles, community participation, enterprise, the global dimension and sustainable development, technology and the media, and creativity and critical thinking can provide a useful steer. What opportunities are there for combining musical performance with science (a study of acoustics and sound waves?); dance and design (integrated exhibitions?); English (music and readings of prose or poetry?); maths (do numbers and music really link together in the way everyone suggests in conversation when they discover you are a music teacher?). Sometimes it may not even be necessary to swap classes and a possible starting point might be simply to include teachers in other subject areas to provide a backdrop for performance work which can help to place it into another context. Could the media teacher outline the requirements and working environment of the music industry in the context of film and television? What are the expectations and timeframes which would help all students to be able to perform in another part of the school? Perhaps this could even be part of an event in the visiting teacher's department? There are many possible approaches that could be developed in this area.

At one high school, cross-curricular working has led to performing arts evenings. These evenings are not for ensemble groups which have been rehearsed by the teacher, but a showcase for all learners to participate. In one such evening with an international flavour, a Year 9 class presented a piece of Gamelan music that they had been working on to accompany a performance using Indonesian-style rod puppets which had been constructed during a design class. Later there was a carnival style presentation using masks and music compositions as well as Chinese singing and dancing and a performance on steel pans. During the interval there was a presentation of Argentinian dance music while sweets were given to the audience, including Argentinian cakes for parents and a goody-bag for children to take away. The evening also included Japanese storytelling, a display of international-influenced art works from the art department and a play from Drama looking at world stories.

The integrated evening event described in the above case study demonstrates exceptional practice as it provides opportunities for all to perform outside the classroom. With careful planning such valuable musical experiences are within the reach of all music departments.

Actively taking students out and about on campus as part of their music lessons can be another progressive approach that raises the profile of music in a school. With the head teacher's permission, why not take groups of students down onto the fields to perform during the summer or take over the hall or canteen to perform at other times? There could be processions to these places involving music-making and, if other students are still in lessons, it is usually fairly straightforward with a little notice to collect a small audience of appreciative support and canteen staff for five or ten minutes, or perhaps even including visitors to the school. This kind of approach is another fresh way to address the Learning Outside the Classroom agenda as well as providing students with a clear aim for the work they are doing in class. Something so simple can have a qualitative impact on the ethos and atmosphere of just another school day.

> At one school, the teacher took her class out and about to play the samba music they had been developing as a whole class. This involved a procession through paths around external buildings and a performance in the staff car park! It gave students a great practical experience to aim for and really raised the profile of music in the school, with noses of students in other classes pressed to the window pane! It was a move supported by the head teacher and a great way to bring performing for all into everyday classroom work.

Extending opportunities for musical performance

Such a model can be further developed into a day of showcasing events across the school, presenting opportunities for all to participate. This does not mean that the music teacher organises numerous ensembles. Instead, the emphasis in this approach is for the students to be encouraged to form small groups and to prepare and rehearse musical items themselves. Everybody who offers anything in any style should be given the chance to perform. It can be surprising how much students relish a task like this and how they rise to the occasion. Generally students are supportive and very enthusiastic to have the chance to hear their friends playing ethnic instruments, rapping, DJ'ing, singing acoustic songs, playing classical instruments and all kinds of fusions, even if not every note is in tune or the performance fully polished!

One approach to encouraging this kind of showcasing was a day of creative events, in which student-led music-making was a strand at one school. This involved setting-up four different stages in different areas of the school at which students performed in a wide variety of styles, as well as running workshops and other more teacher-led opportunities. This was followed up in the summer term by performances on an outdoor stage on the back field of the school. It was striking how many students were keen to be involved in this whose musical talent may not have been immediately obvious and it gave all a real opportunity to contribute.

Working with other schools to develop musical performance opportunities

There is a treasury of musical performance opportunities within a stone's throw of a school in the form of its educational partners. Feeder schools or schools that a school feeds into can be a part of enabling performance opportunities for all. As we discussed in Chapter 2, transition projects of all kinds can help to create some vibrant opportunities. The enthusiastic reaction of primary school children can have a hugely positive impact on high-school students. The variety of transition projects is only limited by our imagination: singing events, rock music projects, composition workshops, DJ'ing and world musical styles can all be good ways in.

One high school established a weekly rock-style workshop for students from a number of local schools. This raised the profile of the music department and effectively demonstrated that in bringing students together, musical enthusiasm was enhanced and this led to real improvements in their musical learning. The emphasis was on working with whatever the students brought to the session, building on and developing these ideas and leading to recording and performance sessions.

Careful planning could also link to the Wider Opportunities work taking place in local primary schools. Students playing similar instruments could be linked and there could be a strong interchange of learning between students of different Key Stages. Importantly, such transition working should not be seen only as something administered to and for the benefit of others; as we saw in Chapter 2, the rewards can also be significant for students from your own school. It is also worth considering inviting other schools to visit your school to enable joint project working, it need not always be you who is doing the travelling!

Working within the local community

There are a host of opportunities within your local community for musical performances. There will be opportunities for performances in community halls and events, a broad range of cultural settings, shopping centres, hospitals and hospices. These will necessitate increased planning, but seek to involve older students in this. Visiting workshop leaders and community musicians can also help to develop projects of this type.

One music department maintains a diverse range of relationships with professional musicians, ensembles and community groups. These have resulted in music performances by school groups, including a big band enhanced by visiting professional musicians and groups from a local music college. These have included presenting work from the school within the local community (at various Lord Mayor's shows), taking groups to perform at the Edinburgh Fringe, as well as international tours.

Using new technologies to facilitate musical networks

New technologies present a range of opportunities for musical performances to be shared, either through recordings or live broadcasts. Exchanges can be established with other schools in other countries to engage with alternative models of curriculum learning. Performing in this case can take place in a virtual environment if the tools exist for this at each school, but at the very least could involve the sharing of performance recordings. This can be another clear goal and aim which students in the music classroom can work towards.

One school used e-mail to add a new dimension to students' understanding of Indian classical music. Through a partnership with an Indian high school, students developed their understanding by asking questions and learning from the Indian students. The Indian students asked about western scales and key systems, as well as learning about other styles of music from their student e-pal. The classes shared video clips of each other performing.

Initiating performance partnerships

As we will see in Chapter 8, performance opportunities for all can be further enhanced through establishing and developing a wide range of partnership working. The performing arts service of the local authority might be the best starting point for exploring the opportunities in your area. There may be partnerships to be developed with arts agencies, universities, orchestras, bands, instrumental makers and others, but always with the aim of facilitating and widening the experience of musical performance for all students.

Summary

All of these ideas about musical performance within and outside the classroom are based on the premise that musical performance is a central element of every student's music education. As will have become apparent, you will need to plan carefully to provide such opportunities. However, it is an achievable goal. It is a statutory part of music curriculum provision and one not to be neglected.

In taking forward these ideas there are benefits for yourself and your students. For the student, the music classroom ceases to be a contained space which is the domain of those considered the musically able. Instead it becomes an exciting area in which they can create and then learn to shape and develop their ideas. Through performing within this space they develop their confidence; outside of this space, they will also begin to discover links with the wider world and with other curriculum subjects for themselves. For the teacher, goals and aspirations are renewed and the challenge of providing effective musical learning experiences for all comes, once again, sharply into focus. Delivering quality performance experiences for all students is a difficult target to achieve and generates its own questions, including how to evaluate, monitor and improve provision. Music teaching is never easy, but it is always engaging. Musical performance provides that essential link between our identity as teachers and musicians, our students' musical lives and the musical lives of our schools, local and national communities. It is worth reconsidering our approach here, and building new networks that give all students the opportunity to enjoy musical performance.

Reflective Questions

1. What steps can I take to broaden my approach to the provision of musical performance opportunities for all students?
2. How can I strengthen the use of performance as a vehicle for learning to develop students' musical understanding?

3. Do I utilise all opportunities to model musical performance rather than relying on verbal explanation?
4. What partnerships can I build in order to develop opportunities for students to perform outside the classroom?

Further Reading 

Fautley, M. (2010) *Assessment in Music Education*. Oxford: Oxford University Press (see in particular Chapter 10: 'Developing classroom performing by the use of assessment').

Fautley, M. and Savage, J. (2010) *Cross-curricular Teaching and Learning in the Secondary School: The Arts*. London: Routledge.

Learning Outside the Classroom: Arts and Creativity. Online at: http://www.lotc.org.uk/Out-and-about-guidance/How-do-we-organise-learning/Framework-for-planning-LOtC-experiences/Where-and-when/Arts-and-creativity (accessed 8 September 2010).

Moran, N. (2009) 'Symphony orchestras, sitars and samba schools – how does community affect musical development?', in H. Coll and A. Lamont (eds), *Sound Progress – Exploring Musical Development.* Matlock: National Association of Music Educators.

Philpott, C. (2001) 'Equality of opportunity and instrumental tuition', in C. Philpott and C. Plummeridge (eds), *Issues in Music Teaching*. London: Routledge.

Reference

Mills, J. and Paynter, J. (eds) (2008) *Thinking and Making: Selections from the Writings of John Paynter on Music in Education*. Oxford: Oxford University Press.

CHAPTER 6

THE ROLE OF MUSIC AND MUSICIANS IN SOCIETY, THE MUSIC INDUSTRY AND INTELLECTUAL PROPERTY RIGHTS

Phil Kirkman

Introduction

In this chapter we will be thinking about the role of music and musicians in society, of the music industry and of artistic and intellectual property rights. We will begin by unpacking the different strands that fall within this topic area. This will allow us to put these strands together in a coherent framework that will help us to present the material in ways which suit our own students, courses and pedagogy. Examples of how strands may be linked to existing units of work are given as we progress. At the same time we must keep in mind that the foundation of our units of work is the Key Concepts and not the Range and Content statements. Thus, while the focus here is on how specific content may be delivered, it should always be in support of the musical learning which flows from the Key Concepts. Topics are not ends in themselves.

Recent changes in music education can be understood as part of a more established trend which we can trace back to the creative approaches of early pioneers such as Dalcroze, Orff and Kodály (Hallam and Creech 2010). In the 1960s and 1970s music educators building on these approaches were keen to move music education towards a *Thinking and Making* curriculum. From this perspective, music education involves building on previous experiences by providing new practical, integrated and collaborative music-making activities. Some writers describe this as a shift away from formulaic traditions that over-emphasised notions of 'expert performers' and adherence to convention.

More recently educators have developed the idea of a 'musical education' (Swanwick 1999; Mills 2005) which emphasises that practical musical experiences are something all people can have. A 'musical' curriculum engages *all* students in 'doing music: making it, creating it, responding to it' (Mills 2005: 2). This approach recognises that our students will come to school with many and varied cultural experiences. These different understandings offer many opportunities for us to foster appreciation and respect for others as we communicate our different musical ideas. Furthermore, understanding how our own perspective has developed may also help to reveal areas for exploration of which we were previously unaware.

The Key Concepts

Working forward from this position it is clear that the Key Concepts build on this wealth of understanding about what good music education looks like. In fact, the notion of music as activity shares a lot in common with Christopher Small's (1998) notion of music as a social activity and not an object. If we see music as something that is 'done', then we can begin to expand our view to include every meaningful act related to music: to 'music' or the act of 'musicking'. Small's idea is particularly helpful for us here, as he provides a perspective that allows us to bring together the seemingly unrelated roles of musical performers, copyright lawyers, printers, the audience and even programme sellers. The trend of developments in music education and the basis of the National Curriculum encourage us to see music as both a *process* and a *product*, the practical activity of making music as well as the tangible outcome of a musical experience.

A framework for understanding music in society

The diversity of music forms that we begin to appreciate when we see practical music experiences as something for all leads us also to see the individual differences between musicians and the distinctions between the contexts in which they work. We can think of these as parts of a society which surrounds and impacts on students, for example through the media, in school or through family and friends.

Yet, while it is clear that society impacts on students' lives, it is also the case that students interact with their context and shape it to suit their own ends.

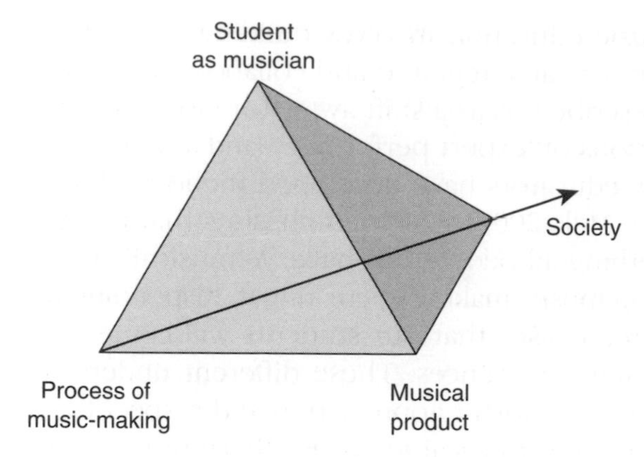

Figure 6.1 Relationships between students as musicians and society

We could represent this as a pyramid on which every point is connected in a direct relationship with every other point: the student, the process of music-making, the musical product and society (Figure 6.1). This representation positions students not just within a context, in this case as consumers of musical products, but also as active participants in the cultural process of music and in the creation and recreation of society as 'musicians'. Society is illustrated as a continued arrow to emphasise that much of society lies outside our own and our students' direct musical experiences.

Having identified our students as musicians and built up a framework of understanding around the place of music in education and society, we can now begin to explore our curriculum topic in more detail. Each point on our pyramid serves as a holder for our ideas. Yet as we progress through each one in turn, we must remember that each aspect relates directly to the others in this constantly changing pattern of relations.

Music in society

Having positioned music education within society, it is now important to consider 'music' itself. The Key Concepts and Key Processes see music as an integrated activity; we perform, we compose, we listen, we collaborate. Each aspect cannot be separated because as we perform we necessarily listen to our performance and create new interpretations as we work with other musicians. If we neglect any aspect of this structure we risk losing all meaningful learning. At the same time, if we focus solely on the process of music-making and never allow students to achieve quality in their musical products then we place in jeopardy what it means to make progress as musicians.

Copyright law as a window into music in society

We may find that copyright law is helpful in the classroom when trying to develop students' awareness of these concepts in music. The distinction between music as a cultural product and as a process is seen in the way copyright law distinguishes between the rights that relate to a 'work' and the rights of a 'performer'. There are essentially two different types of music copyright. Compositions, scores, lyrics and artwork are all covered by the traditional copyright (usually written as ©). In contrast, the recording of a musical work itself is also protected by copyright (written as ℗). In this way music copyright law makes provision for recordings of music for which the copyright has expired (in the UK this is the life of the author plus 70 years). While such a work was initially covered by traditional copyright, the performance is recognised as an artistic contribution in itself. Thus the performer is protected by copyright law for 50 years after the year of the performance or 50 years from the date of release. (This figure may vary depending on national laws.)

Copyright law gives us a neat way into thinking about music-making and the result of music-making as two connected ideas. It helps us to distinguish between the rights held by the author of a musical composition and the rights of a performer. Importantly, it also allows students to see the connection between 'doing music' – what might appear to be abstract exercises that form a musical process of working – and 'the music' – as a 'product' or 'recording'.

Working forwards from this point, we can now see that any discussion about the role of music in society must include its function as the products of artistic and creative endeavours. Yet it must also consider the processes of music-making, which include a vast array of related trades and responsibilities. Blacking (1973) provides an extended discussion of these complementary roles, highlighting the close connection between societies, culture and music-making as each forms, informs and reforms the other. His first two chapters serve to illustrate the interaction between sounds as something that can be organised by humans to form music (product). In contrast, his final two chapters demonstrate how we see the structures and processes of a society in its cultural artefacts, one of which is music. He shows how the process of music-making can be a key part of the way a society organises itself and passes on tradition. It is straightforward to see how this translates into our tradition: weddings, birthdays, funerals, feasts or celebrations like Easter and Christmas, coronations, even sporting events. An interesting modern application is the way music is used by the media to denote a particular product or programme or in film to indicate mood or character.

We can add this to our framework by placing copyright on the bottom edge of our pyramid. In this way we show how copyright law underpins the

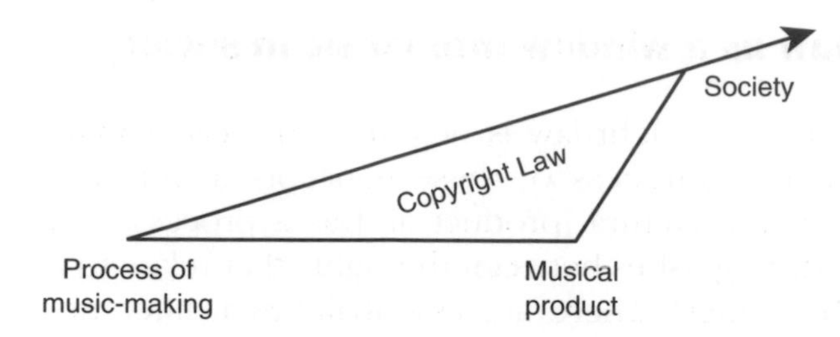

Figure 6.2 Copyright as central to the interaction between music and society

interaction between musical processes, products and their place in society (see Figure 6.2).

In the classroom

This approach to the role of music in society is twofold. Music on the one hand is sound that has been organised as a means of personal expression, for entertainment and as a commercial product. On the other hand, music is a constant process of production and reproduction of cultural artefacts that reflect and influence the organisation of society. In the classroom this gives us two complementary ways of working that together form a perspective for deepening students' critical and cultural understanding: (1) working on a 'piece' and (2) 'doing' music in a context. Below is an example of how these ideas might feature in a unit of work. The content is left intentionally broad to allow adjustment for the individual needs of different contexts and students.

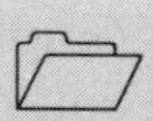

Students are introduced to a variety of pieces in order to explore expressions of war and peace across time and place:

- *War and Peace* (Prokofiev);
- 'The Last Post';
- Second World War songs;
- film music, e.g. soundtracks from *Platoon. The Patriot*;
- 'Born in the USA' (Bruce Springsteen). 'War Pigs' (Black Sabbath). 'Bullet in the Blue Sky'(U2);
- 'I-Feel-Like-I'm-Fixin'-to-Die Rag' (Country Joe).

The pupils investigate how these musical products arose from events in society and how they impacted upon future events. Did copyright law alter their impact at the time? The pupils develop their understanding of how music is used to build community (through collective singing, lyrics, events). The pupils develop a class 'war and peace' song.

The musician in society, the music industry

Having identified copyright as the building block of our understanding of music, we must now begin to unpack the three sides of our pyramid simultaneously. We have seen that copyright law can help to define music as a process, which is called a 'performance'. At the same time, we have also noted that we cannot assume 'musician' necessarily means 'performer'. Thus students working practically as musicians could be arranging, recording, performing management responsibilities, repairing and designing instruments, or working in radio, venue hire, sales, transport, education, church music or journalism.

As well as allowing the distinction between product and process to be neatly explained, copyright law can also help us to see many of the various roles that 'musicians' (as those involved in the process of making music) may occupy (see Table 6.1). This is by no means an exhaustive list and there may be many more roles that students can identify as fruitful avenues for inquiry.

The UK copyright service identifies seven different types of 'work' that are protected by copyright law: Musical, Literary, Dramatic, Artistic, Typographical, Sound recording and Films. Using these as starting points we can start to see niches into which different people fit who are involved in the process of making and doing music. This is shown in Table 6.1. As well as revealing the vast number of employment roles within the industry, this exercise helps to remind us that it is not just music copyright law that impacts on work in the music industry. In addition we may wish to add several roles that do not necessarily involve creating copyright material:

- *consumers*: perhaps a neglected group but the financial 'power' of this group can define the scope of what is produced;
- *amateur musicians and students* (separated from professional musicians as their approach to issues such as copyright and financial reward may be quite different);
- *support industries*: catering, printing, electronic engineering, lighting.

In the classroom

From the list in Table 6.1 it is clear that the most easily defined role of 'musician', that of performer, is only a small part of the process of music in society. Identifying the different stakeholders in this way gives us a good starting point when considering the value of role-play in promoting classroom learning. Below are examples of lessons that bring together these ideas.

Table 6.1 Types of copyright work and related roles in society

Types of copyright work produced	Examples of copyright works	Areas of employment	'Musician' as one involved in the music process
Literary	Song lyrics, manuscripts, manuals, computer programs, commercial documents, leaflets, newsletters and articles, etc.	Business and management	Personal manager, booking agent, concert promoter, music publisher, professional manager, business manager
		Publicity	Public relations, counsellor, public relations trainee, publicist, assistant publicist
Dramatic	Plays, dance, performances, etc.	Music tours	Tour coordinator, road manager, tour publicist, sound technician, advance person
		Arenas, facilities, halls and clubs	Concert hall manager, stage manager, resident sound technician, nightclub manager
		Radio	Music director, disc jockey
Musical	Recordings and scores	Orchestras, symphonies, etc.	Conductor, section leader, section member, managing director, orchestra manager, business manager, director of development, director of public relations, subscriptions and ticket service director, director of educational activities, personnel director, orchestra music librarian
		Talent and writing	Record group, floor show band, dance band, session musician, background vocalist, songwriter
		Church music	Choir director, cantor, organist
Artistic	Photography, painting, technical drawings/diagrams, logos	Instrument repair, restoration and design	Music instrument builder/designer, instrument repair and restoration specialist
Typographical	Magazines, periodicals, etc.	Journalism	Music journalist
Sound recording	May be recordings of other copyright works, e.g. musical and literary	Recording and the music business	Artists and repertoire coordinator, artists and repertoire administrator, promotion staff, staff publicist, artist relations and development representative, consumer researcher, advertising account executive, regional sales manager, salesperson, field merchandiser, intern, campus representative, arranger, record producer, recording engineer, recording studio set-up worker, orchestrator, copyist
Film	Broadcasts and cable programmes	TV and film	Production sound recordist, foley artist, sound editor, sound mixer, composer
Various		Retail and wholesale	Music shop manager, music shop salesperson, record shop or department manager, record shop clerk, instrument sales representative, rack jobber, website manager
		Education	Music supervisor, college, conservatory or university music educator, secondary music teacher, primary music specialist, instrumental teacher, music therapist, music librarian

As part of the unit of work on 'War and Peace', students take on the role of three different 'musicians' at the time their piece was composed. Students could take on different roles within the music industry: as artists who are striving to get their 'message' out to a public; as journalists and publicists who are looking for copy and commenting on current events; as booking agents trying to find the right engagement for their artist; or as a concert hall manager looking to ensure their venue turns a profit. There are more than enough possible roles for each student to take on an individual role as part of a whole-class improvisational activity which examines the context of a particular musical stimulus. Key Concepts to focus on might include creativity, cultural understanding and critical understanding. They perform their role as if they were there at the time. They consider the question: How does your role change your perspective on the piece?

Another example is use the work of a producer such as Sir George Martin, to consider his impact on the sound of the Beatles. Practical activities might involve reworking some Beatles music from a different perspective, for example a music venue wanting to publicise a concert, a journalist looking to portray the Beatles' working-class background or a producer looking to reintroduce their music to a new generation.

If we turn once again to our model we can distribute the roles identified in Table 6.1 in different ways around our framework. We can then more easily consider the ways in which these roles interact with music in society. For example, workers in business and management or publicity may choose to prioritise the interaction between society and a musical product. In contrast, orchestras or church musicians may decide to focus more on the interaction between society and the process of music-making. Finally, many workers in education and in the recording industry may approach music with the interaction between a musical product and the process of music as a priority. This is shown in Figure 6.3. Of course, each student in role may choose any of the alternative perspectives. Our model is simply a tool to encourage students to consider how they might behave in each of these different roles.

The classroom and music in society

One of the big challenges in the classroom is to provide rich varied contexts for authentic music-making. Of course, students' own musical histories can help with this as their experiences position them with a tacit understanding of many aspects of music in society. An easy example is the way in which

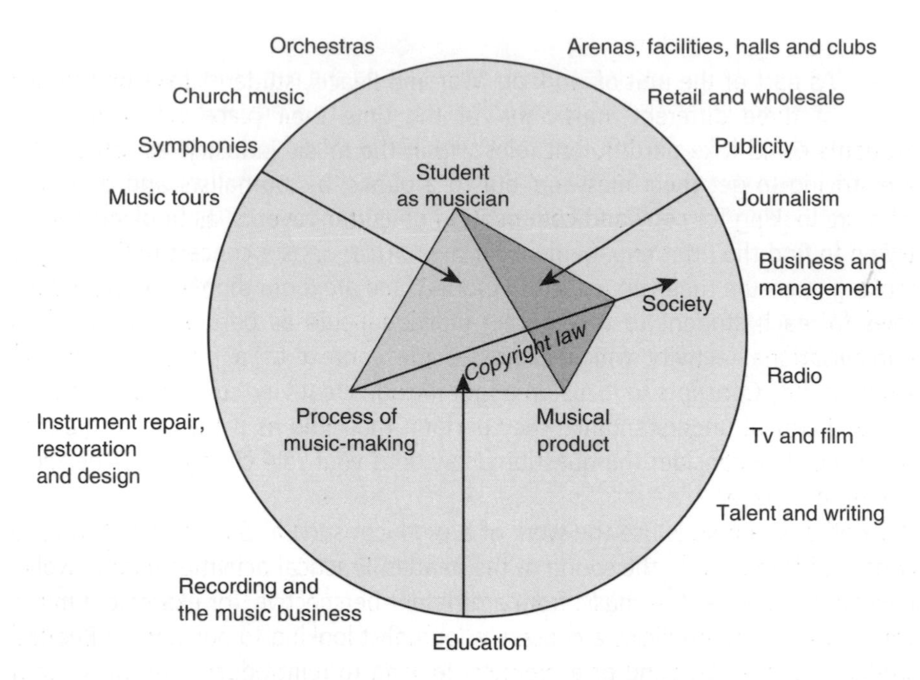

Figure 6.3 Musical roles and possible relationships with music and society

reality television shows such as *X Factor*, *Britain's Got Talent* and *Pop Idol* have opened the process of selecting artists and repertoire to the public. In this case our role as teachers is to bring these hidden understandings to the surface.

A further way of addressing the challenge is to work forward from our understanding of the different roles of musicians in society. Authentic music-making in society seeks to balance the creativity of an individual with the needs of society. A successful musician must balance their own experience with that of their audience. If we consider a musical tradition from the standpoint of any of the 'musician' roles identified above we can begin to ask new questions of the music and encounter it from new perspectives. Put another way, by suspending our own history and preferences we can walk in the shoes of any musician. Once we have used our imagination to see music and its place in a society from the perspective of another we can then bring this understanding back into our own environment, so enriching our own musical understanding. For example, students could evaluate their composition from the perspective of a booking agent seeking to promote their client. Using this evaluation, students could then improve their work to make it more commercially attractive to a club owner or concert promoter. The following example shows how this might look as part of our unit on 'War and Peace'.

Pupils begin work as a composer writing on the theme of 'War and Peace'. They are given a choice to compose for a film score, a documentary or a song for a demo CD. When they have finished a draft, the pupils are asked to change character and write an evaluation of the piece from three different perspectives. They then refine and develop their compositions further based on their evaluations.

Digital resources

It is clear that covering this ground with a full class of different students is no small task. Yet, because a musical education has its roots in practical activity, digital technology offers several avenues to explore that may prove fruitful when used in a busy classroom. At the same time we should remember that digital technologies are now frequently used across the whole of society as a way of working with music. In this way it is hard to see how many school music-making contexts could avoid the use of digital technologies and remain relevant in today's society. Each of the following can be integrated into a unit of work alongside the range and content discussed above and provides opportunities to extend existing practice beyond the walls of the classroom and into real-life music-making.

The mashup

http://www.mashup-charts.com
This is a constantly changing resource of the latest popular music songs that have been remixed as mashups. A mashup combines music from two or more sources to produce a new work. This site is useful for stimulus material and as a way into a niche popular music community. Finished work can be shared online.

http://opensourcecinema.org/project/rip2.0
The open source cinema project is a resource for students to share, remix, recycle and blog. Students can download, edit and use the films as stimulus material with no worries about copyright. There is a built in remix editor that can be used to mix clips online if the school network can handle it. This site provides great video that is thought-provoking. It is split up into manageable chunks. Also, the project provides the means to upload and talk about your work. So, for example, you could use Chapter 1 as a

whole-class introduction to the project and as stimulus for a conversation about copyright.

Both sites provide opportunities to introduce copyright and the distinction between music as a product and a process. They might be good stimulus material for learning about the tension between new music forms, file sharing and the law.

Online sharing

http://soundcloud.com/
Soundcloud was founded in 2007 as a way to move around large music files. It now hosts many musical works as well as being a Facebook-like community in which to talk about music and share ideas. Many professional musicians are on here as well as amateurs, students and bands.

http://www.numu.org.uk/
A safe, education-based resource for young people to connect, publish and share their original music.

Both these resources highlight the different possible views of music. They can be used to highlight how communities grow around different music forms.

Online music-making communities

http://www.jamstudio.com/Studio/index.htm
Jamstudio is a Flash-based 'online music factory' that feels a bit like a cross between eJay and Band-in-a-Box. Several recent articles have highlighted the benefits of these technologies and their usefulness in classroom situations. This program could be helpful as a template or starting point for a 'groove' or structure to import into a sequencer. Students could record their own ideas over the top and even remove the mp3 once they have recorded all their ideas. This is particularly useful as a complement to informal learning practice.

http://www.noteflight.com/login
Noteflight is a website that allows you to create, store, listen to, print, search and share notated music online. In a similar way to Jamstudio, you can create your music online and then share what you have written. The community aspect of noteflight means that students can work collaboratively – even internationally.

Summary

The different themes arising from our topic of music and musicians in society can be put together to form the four points of a pyramid: the musical product, the musical process, students as musicians and society. Doing this allows us to extract themes that can be integrated into existing units of work or which can be used to form the basis of new units. In so doing, we can encourage students to reflect on the quality of musical experience, copyright, the roles of musicians and the nature of the music industry. As we do this, authentic contexts for music-making will emerge as a natural part of the process of inquiry.

It has never been more urgent that we help to bring about an awareness of the power of music to form and transform people. The changing nature of much of the music in our society and current issues of ownership and copyright provide many opportunities to stimulate music-making. Music represents, reinvents and develops the bedrock structures of society. This is not to say that we have carte blanche to decide what is good music; what may be helpful in one context will probably differ widely from what will be suitable in another. What we appreciate may well stand apart from what our students value. Instead, working from new understandings of music and musicians in society, students can begin to address the much deeper and broader area of understanding about what constitutes a 'musical experience'. This is ultimately what must be fostered and developed within our classrooms and with our students.

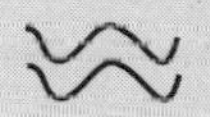

Reflective Questions

1. How can I adapt existing units of work to focus on the musical process, the musical product, students as musicians and music in society?
2. How can I develop authentic contexts for music-making?

Further Reading

http://www.copyrightservice.co.uk (accessed 8 October 2010); http://www.licensing-copyright.org (accessed 8 October 2010). The UK Copyright Service has a series of factsheets about copyright available online. A helpful leaflet about copyright in school can be found at licensing-copyright.org. This helpful website also includes a series of links that will provide plenty of details about the inner workings of copyright law.

http://www.mantleoftheexpert.com (accessed 8 October 2010). A good resource for those interested in using role-play in teaching. Based on a pedagogy established by Dorothy Heathcote, it is pupil-led and involves the imaginary formation of a community. This website has a wealth of material on the strengths of role-play, how to set up a learning context and how to maintain students' involvement. This approach is especially useful if dealing with the music industry as a complete topic.

Many helpful links to online resources can also be found on the BBC Learning website: http://www.bbc.co.uk/learning/subjects/music.shtml (accessed 8 October 2010).

References

Blacking, J. (1973) *How Musical is Man?* Seattle, WA: Washington University Press.

Hallam, S. and Creech, A. (2010) *Music Education in the 21st Century in the United Kingdom: Achievements, Analysis and Aspirations*. London: Institute of Education.

Mills, J. (2005) *Music in the School.* Oxford: Oxford University Press.

Small, C. (1998) *Musicking: The Meanings of Performing and Listening.* Lebanon, NH: University Press of New England.

Swanwick, K. (1999) *Teaching Music Musically.* London: Routledge.

CHAPTER 7

USING MUSIC TECHNOLOGY FOR MUSICAL PERFORMANCE

David Ashworth

Introduction

In this chapter, we explore the possibilities of using music technologies in live musical performance settings. Music technologies can include specific pieces of hardware (e.g. synthesisers, samplers or sound processors), software (e.g. Ableton Live, Cubase, etc.) or other technologies (e.g. Nintendo DS Lite, Sony PlayStations, etc.). Like any traditional musical instrument, each piece of music technology will have its own strengths and weaknesses. But using these types of technology in musical performance often leads to refreshing new instrumental combinations, where pupils can experiment with new textures and timbres. It can be genuinely creative, because the music usually has to be devised and improvised. This, in turn, helps our pupils to develop the essential skills required for music performance and become more fully rounded musicians.

Firstly, we consider where and how this approach to music-making fits into the National Curriculum framework. The main drivers are:

- to provide opportunities and pointers for more creative music-making using technology;

- to encourage a more 'authentic' approach, where what goes on in the classroom might reflect more closely some aspects of music-making in the world beyond the school gates;
- to make music-making more inclusive, by encouraging and providing a platform for those students who may lack some of the skills or aptitude for more traditional approaches.

Secondly, we will consider strategies for using ICT in this way in a range of contexts. These strategies are fully supported by case study examples drawn from our recent work with teachers in schools across the United Kingdom.

The conclusion summarises the key principles and approaches discussed in the chapter and their relevance within the broader picture of music education. The benefits and implications of this approach and the ways in which they can be used to frame teachers' future practice are also given consideration.

Music technology and the National Curriculum

Using technology to aid processes of musical performance provides the potential to support a range of requirements in the National Curriculum. In this section, we show how information and communication technology (ICT) for live musical performance maps onto these requirements.

The first Key Concept statement (Integration of Practice) stresses the importance of participating, collaborating and working with others because music is essentially a social experience:

> Participating, collaborating and working with others as musicians, adapting to different musical roles and respecting the values and benefits others bring to musical learning. (QCA 2007: 180)

Using music technology in live performance provides students with the same ensemble and performing skills as other more traditional approaches might bring. The Range and Content statements refer explicitly to music technologies:

> The use of music technologies to create, manipulate and refine sounds. (QCA 2007: 183)

The explanatory notes provide some helpful clarification:

> Use of music technologies: This includes the use of ICT and music technologies to control and structure sound in performing and composing activities, and in developing pupils' own ideas within and beyond the classroom.

This statement makes reference to performance activities in a range of contexts including online performance events. Furthermore, students are now encouraged to use music technologies to not only control and structure sound in composing activities, but also in performance.

This idea of technology in performance is also reinforced in the Curriculum Opportunities section of the document where pupils should be offered the opportunity to:

> Develop individual performance skills, both vocal and instrumental, including the use of music technology. (QCA 2007: 184)

Learning and teaching principles and approaches

As we have seen throughout this book, the best models of music teaching and learning integrate the key musical processes of performance, composition, listening, reviewing and evaluating rather than thinking of them in isolation from each other. At a very practical level, in the past it was common for classroom music to be completely independent from the instrumental teaching provision/school ensemble activity. Chapter 5 argues for the barriers between these to be broken, and in schools where these two areas have been brought together, we have seen that these strengthen and support each other. Now we have a third element in the classroom – ICT. In many schools this is regarded as a discrete activity and is often only found at KS4 and above. This chapter looks at possible ways of integrating ICT into traditional classroom music-making throughout the secondary school.

There are five typical scenarios for the use of ICT in performance which can all be used in different teaching and learning curriculum contexts.

1. Using technology to create a backing track

This can be useful for students who want to work on their own or for small groups as a way of 'expanding' the size of their ensemble. It can also be a good way to provide access to instrumental timbres that they cannot make themselves. Students can feel supported and uplifted by a good backing track. Critics of this approach may think of it as 'cheating', but a significant degree of musicianship is required to create the tracks – and to perform with them.

A small classical guitar ensemble was conscious that when they performed alongside other groups in school concerts, they made a quiet sound that was limited in tonal variety. Two members of the group used Acid

(Continued)

(Continued)

Express to create an 'ambient soundtrack' that could be used to provide an atmospheric underscoring to one of their pieces based on a South American theme. Because of the 'drifting' nature of the backing, there was no requirement to synchronise with a given beat, although sectional changes had to be observed. They were able to rework their guitar piece to include some semi-improvised passages and some points where the backing played solo sections as interludes. Some simple visual projections were added to heighten the atmosphere in the performance.

Loop-based sequencer software applications such as eJay and Sony Acid can be used to create multitrack backings for live performers. Hip hop artists and rappers will often utilise this type of software to put together their backings (or beats). It is quite common for a rapper to commission a third party to produce beats for him/her. This could provide the basis for some collaborative classroom work bringing together the confident extrovert performer and the computer whizz kid! Pupils can create and/or record original material into these frameworks and also make use of royalty free samples.

At an after-school computer club, a small group of students created some 'techno samba' pieces for a joint performance with the school drumming group. They were asked to concentrate on some of the more esoteric Latin sounds which would complement rather than compete with the live percussion. Highly rhythmic sections were interspersed with freer-flowing, ambient sections which gave some of the percussionists the freedom to explore short improvisations where they were not chained to the metronomic beat created by the computer. The recordings were also passed on to a dance group in the school who prepared some Latin dance-style movements. The whole thing was put together to create a stunningly rich audiovisual performance.

Alternatively, MIDI backings can be created in auto accompaniment programs such as Band-in-a-Box and used in performance using karaoke software such as vanBasco.

A primary school set up a local-global project on trees – looking at trees in their locality and the Brazilian rainforests. Part of the project was on songwriting. When they had written the words for their songs, they used the software program Words & Music to help create melodies for their lyrics which could be saved as MIDI files. The MIDI files were imported into Band-in-a-Box and appropriate accompaniments were created where consideration was given to style, tempo, key, etc. For performance, the files were played in vanBasco so that the lyrics could be scrolled as the children sang. This helped the younger performers who were struggling to remember the order of verses/choruses, etc. Appropriate video backdrops (mainly trees!) were displayed behind the lyrics to provide an effective focal point for the performance. Some live instruments were added to some of the songs.

There are many examples in the outside world of this approach to music-making that go well beyond the world of karaoke bars. Steve Reich has, of course, used a 'DIY backing tape' approach many times, particularly in his 'Counterpoint' series of commissioned works. From the world of rock and pop music, listen to Pete Townshend's use of a synthesiser in 'Baba O'Riley'.

2. Solo performance

There are times when a student will have to, or will want to, work alone. They may want to be totally in control of a composition/performance or other musicians may not be available to work with. This can take one of two forms.

A performance using technology specifically intended for this purpose

Typical software applications such as Ableton Live or Audiomulch are now being explored for use in schools. In contrast to many other software sequencers, Ableton Live is designed to be an instrument for live performances as well as a tool for composing and arranging. It is also used for the mixing of tracks by DJs, as it offers a suite of controls for beatmatching, crossfading and other effects used by turntablists, and was one of the first music applications to automatically beat match songs. These applications allow the user to assemble a range of sounds (any combination of pre-recorded samples, signal generators and live feeds) and combine and manipulate them in real time. Sounds can be triggered individually or in groups and processed using an array of sound effects.

A young 'Musical Futures' band were having trouble creating the kind of sound they wanted. They were attempting a cover version of a song by New Order which required a very 'robotic' drum sound. The band's drummer lacked the technical skill to do this convincingly. Since they were working with the usual drums/bass/keyboard line-up, they were unable to produce some of the more esoteric synthesised sounds of the original track. They were encouraged to use a Mixman DM2* device to address these challenges. One of the band members used this device to provide a steady, convincing percussion track to which she was able to add an impressive array of synthesised and processed sounds. The drummer moved on to playing hand-held percussion to help the band retain a live feel.

*The Mixman DM2 has a pair of 'turntables' which allow the user to trigger, mix and combine up to 16 sampled sounds at a time. These sounds can be sonically altered in real time using a joystick to control various filtering parameters. Users can work with pre-recorded sounds or assign their own samples to the trigger pads.

Hardware applications include DJ technology or loop samplers such as the Roland RC50. External MIDI controllers can be used to give greater performance control when working with computers. Typically, these will have a range of rotary knobs, sliders and trigger pads which can be mapped directly onto the parameters the performer may wish to control. Some MIDI keyboards also have controllers. In addition, gaming devices are now being used as MIDI controllers (Hand2Hand and Nintendo Wiis are two notable examples). Many young people already own these types of controllers and have already developed considerable skill in using them in other contexts.

Acoustic instrument sounds which are processed or 'treated' using technology

An early example of this approach (not electronic, but still technological) is John Cage's use of a prepared piano. Harold Budd and Brian Eno have further explored the use of electronic processing of a solo piano. Other well known musicians who have experimented in this way to great effect include John Martyn, Evan Parker, John Zorn and Robert Fripp. This sort of approach can act as a real spur to young players who are playing some of the more traditional instruments where it can be hard to produce a convincing solo performance with a full, rich 'contemporary' sound.

A GCSE student composed and performed a solo cello piece. She was satisfied with it, but felt that there was 'something lacking'. After seeing a YouTube clip where a cellist demonstrates using a cello with a delay pedal, she decided to investigate further. She borrowed a unit from a guitarist friend and after a short process of trial and error came up with some effective additional textural layers. This added another dimension to the music giving the sound a more 'haunting quality'.

A more recent manifestation of soloist with technology can be found in beatboxing, which uses amplification and equalisation to process the human voice to sound like an array of percussion instruments. There are some interesting clips on the Internet showing beatboxers working with a conventional choir. Perhaps this is something you might like to investigate?

Two secondary schools came together for the challenge of performing a set of songs from *Sgt Pepper's Lonely Hearts Club Band*. In trying to capture the sound of the album as closely as possible, several techniques were employed.

For the opening two tracks ('Sgt Pepper's' and 'With a Little Help from My Friends') the distinctive audience chatter, applause and laughter sounds were located as royalty-free samples from the Internet and triggered during the performance from a laptop running Soundplant. 'Being for the Benefit of Mr Kite' contains some *musique concrète* material using a collage of manipulated fairground sounds. A selection was located from various sources and layered to give a fair approximation of the Beatles' original. Playing the keyboard through a phaser also helped to recreate this unique sound. 'When I'm Sixty Four' contains some short passages for chimes. These were played using a keyboard synthesiser preset.

3. ICT performance ensembles

In addition to laptop orchestras and ensembles, performance groups could include some or all of the following: electronic keyboard, drum machine, samplers, sound processor, computer-generated material, MIDI controllers, sequencers and DJ decks.

These ensembles are by their very nature, resource intensive and may be beyond the reach of some schools. However, there are some possibilities here which may be of interest. Students may have access to some equipment at home which they could be encouraged to bring into schools (check health and safety implications – the equipment may need Portable Appliance Testing (PAT)). Junkshops, eBay and similar sites can be a great source of outdated equipment. D&T departments in schools might welcome the opportunity to engage in a collaborative project where students design and build some appropriate instruments or sound-making devices.

An Internet search will unearth video clips of laptop orchestras etc. of varying quality and interest.

4. Mixed ensembles

This is probably a more realistic approach for schools to adopt in classroom teaching situations where technical resources are limited. Traditional instruments can be mixed with technological applications to provide a highly flexible unit for performance and composition. Examples of groups working in this area include the Kronos Quartet, New Order, The Who (especially the *Quadrophenia* album and performances) and Evan Parker's electro acoustic ensemble.

David Bedford's recent work *The Wreck of the Titanic* makes effective use of ICT in live performance. This large-scale work is scored for string ensemble, youth orchestra, choirs and primary-school musicians. In this episodic work there are 'windows' where pupils are invited to compose additional layers of sounds to a series of composition briefs. They are encouraged to make use of appropriate music technology in the composition and performance of these interludes. For the premiere performances, students from Liverpool and Lancashire used sound editing software to create a bank of processed sounds which could be triggered and layered using a sampler in performance. Morse signals relayed from the *Titanic* were recreated and manipulated using MIDI to generate further melodic material. Sound processors were also used to facilitate real-time processing of acoustic sounds.

The Kronos Quartet's David Harrington (2010) is quoted as saying:

> I'm most interested in bringing elements – sounds, musical feelings and colours – into the realm of what we call the string quartet that have never been there before, I feel fortunate every day that the vocabulary keeps getting larger.

A good example from the Kronos commissioned repertoire is 'Tashweesh', a collaboration between the Kronos Quartet and a Palestinian electronic collective called Ramallah Underground. As the fuzzy beats and 'staticky' notes of Ramallah Underground's half of the composition form the backdrop, the strings pick and pluck their way through an intro that threatens to turn into hip hop but never actually does.

A secondary school used elements of music technology incorporated into an 'acoustic' performance using real-time sound processing and working with a laptop computer as a musical instrument. The musicians using the technology were playing alongside a guitarist, percussionist, saxophonist and keyboard player. Using a laptop running AudioMulch and a USB MIDI controller, they created an 'instrument' that gives the user control over elements of pitch, duration, dynamics and timbre. The laptop musician sat with the rest of the ensemble and responded to the visual and audio cues that arose in the ensemble performance.

They used independent amplification, located close to where they were performing, so that the players became associated with the sounds they were generating. Balancing the sound was done by ensuring that students listened to each other and worked together, so that the 'technical' musician developed the same listening and ensemble skills as the 'acoustic' performers.

5. Multimedia and cross-curricular approaches

Although music has usually been taught as a discrete subject in the curriculum, as we saw in Chapter 3, outside the school it rarely stands in this isolation. For example, contemporary music is often presented in a multimedia context combined with elements of dance or video. In other historical contexts and cultures, music is inextricably linked with elements of dance, drama or ritual. As we have argued in Chapter 3, to make music education relevant to a wide range of contexts in which young people encounter music outside school, many of which are multimedia, some traditional subject barriers may need to be broken down. As we have seen, there are many opportunities for working with music in cross-curricular ways, and music produced digitally significantly increases the range of possibilities.

A composition and performance project at a secondary school involved elements of art, mathematics and music. Students analysed the works of the painter John Wells and discovered that there was a mathematical basis

(Continued)

(Continued)

underlying the structure of many of his paintings, making use of prime numbers and patterns based on the Fibonacci series.

Music Generator was used to translate some of this mathematical data into musical fragments or motifs for use as building blocks in the final composition. Various software applications were used for developing and arranging the musical materials generated in this way. Sections of the paintings were scanned and animated using Microsoft Photo Story and these video projections served as a backdrop for the performance. These projections also functioned as a graphic score, providing a series of cues for those musicians performing live.

Summary

Using music technologies to facilitate processes of musical performance in the classroom has a number of benefits for our students.

Firstly, it affords our students who are primarily interested in music technology the opportunity to collaborate with others and further develop their musicianship skills. It makes teaching and learning music more inclusive and engaging. It opens performance opportunities to those who do not have traditional instrumental playing skills (for whatever reason) and makes strong connections with the music many of our pupils enjoy.

Secondly, because virtually no notated repertoire exists for using ICT in performance, it encourages aural development and creative approaches to developing a repertoire. It also facilitates music-making in cross-arts and cross-curricular contexts because it is relatively easy to integrate music produced digitally with other media. Given that a significant amount of music is now distributed and broadcast over the Internet, using digital technologies allows pupils to engage with online opportunities for composition and musical performance.

Using ICT in this way often works well in a personalised learning environment, where students are working on their own composition/projects individually or in small groups. Problems of limited resources can then be overcome by allowing the students access to them on a pre-booking or rota basis. This approach has been going on in art departments for many years but is possibly something new for music departments.

Students will get far more from this approach if they are aware of the possibilities. Some targeted research and related listening is going to be essential. The Wikipedia entry on electronic music is a useful starting point in providing an overview of the development and application over a range of genres and styles. Teachers are advised to build up a library of listening resources; the examples included in this chapter would make a useful starting point.

Reflective Questions

1. *What about the costs associated with the use of ICT in live performance? Is it affordable?*
   Some of the software applications mentioned here are available in freeware/shareware form. Look out for cost-effective site licence deals and student/lite editions which often have almost as much functionality as the full product. It is possible to download trial versions from some of the websites. It is worth shopping around the music education catalogues/websites for deals on hardware and great savings can often be made on sites such as eBay if you are happy to buy used equipment.
2. *Are these technologies easy to use?*
   Look out for video or Flash tutorials either bundled with the product or on the maker's websites. Some computer music magazines provide effective tutorials which are available for download from their websites. It is possible that there may be members of staff or older students who have some experience/expertise in using this equipment. Don't be afraid of making use of their knowledge! Another good strategy is to learn the basics of the application first and work within these limitations, gradually adding further skills over time.
3. *What about set up time?*
   Computer-based technology applications can be set up relatively quickly. It is often merely a case of plugging a laptop into a small portable amplifier/monitor. Many USB devices do not require a separate power supply and most are 'plug and play'.
4. *What about reliability?*
   Apple Macintosh and Windows XP operating systems are highly stable and cope well with most music applications. In addition, most modern computers have a specification which can cope comfortably with the handling of audio processing. If you are thinking about working over a school network, it would be advisable to discuss possible issues with your ICT support team.
5. *What about repertoire?*
   You are unlikely to find any notated repertoire for music produced in this context. The process encourages the use of original composition and improvisation or the adaptation of existing arrangements. A lot can be learnt adopting an aural approach and by listening to artists who have effectively harnessed the use of technology in their work. Refer to *Electrifying Music* (Ashworth 2007) for some suggestions.

Further Reading 

Ashworth, D. (2007) *Electrifying Music: A Guide to Using ICT in Music Education*. London: Paul Hamlyn Foundation. Online at: http://media.musicalfutures.org.uk/documents/resource/27243/Electrifying_Music_Bw.pdf (accessed 22 November 2010).

Becta Hard to Teach Materials: http://www.name.org.uk/projects/becta/hard-teach (accessed 22 November 2010).

Teaching Music: http://www.teachingmusic.org.uk (accessed 22 November 2010).

Teachnet: http://www.teachnet-uk.org.uk/2006%20Projects/Music-Sounds_of_Kandinsky/index.htm (accessed 22 November 2010).

References

Ashworth, D. (2007) *Electrifying Music: A Guide to Using ICT in Music Education*. London: Paul Hamlyn Foundation. Online at: http://media.musicalfutures.org.uk/documents/resource/27243/Electrifying_Music_Bw.pdf (accessed 22 November 2010).

Harrington, D. (2010) Online at: http://soundinsights.carnegiehall.org/2010/01/kronos-quartet-shaking-things-up.html (accessed 8 October 2010).

Qualifications and Curriculum Authority (2007) *Music: Programme of Study for Key Stage 3 and Attainment Target*. London: QCA.

CHAPTER 8

WORKING WITH A RANGE OF MUSICIANS

Jayne Price

Introduction

In Chapter 6, we discussed the increased emphasis in the music curriculum on connecting students to the 'real world' of music and the role of music and musicians in society. One way of developing students' understanding further is to provide opportunities for them to work with a range of musicians who can talk to them about their professional lives, engage them in musical processes which link to 'real-life' briefs and give them access to high-quality professional practice.

At the same time, providing the range and breadth of music implied in the curriculum can be a challenge for music teachers. Developing relationships with community musicians can provide authentic musical experiences which enhance students' cultural understanding and provide teachers with opportunities to work in areas that they may be unfamiliar with as well as enhance or refresh aspects of their subject knowledge.

In this chapter, we will explore different ways of working with musicians and outline the potential benefits for students, teachers and musicians. We will consider how to plan collaborative projects in school, and use case studies from our work with teachers to show how a broad range of musicians can be used in the classroom to develop and enhance the music curriculum.

Curriculum framework

The National Curriculum outlines that students should develop their understanding of music by working collaboratively together and with others as musicians. 'Participating, collaborating and working with others as musicians, adapting to musical roles and respecting the values and benefits that others bring to musical learning' is part of the key concept of Integration of Practice (QCA 2007: 180).

As part of this process, students should be given the opportunity to 'work with a range of musicians and watch and listen to live musical performances where possible, to extend their musical learning' (QCA 2007: 184). Potentially, working with a range of musicians can provide opportunities for teachers to broaden the music programme of study and to develop students' understanding of musical conventions, processes and devices from a variety of diverse musical styles, genres and traditions.

The guidance in the music programme of study makes it clear that the range of musicians could include instrumental tutors, community musicians, professional artists, amateur musicians, students from peer groups and other groups within the school and also web-based learning opportunities.

Across the National Curriculum, schools are encouraged to provide a range of 'compelling learning experiences' for students. These activities are intended to connect learning in school to the world beyond the classroom, to broaden horizons and raise students' aspirations, and to provide contexts which challenge students and encourage them to step outside their comfort zones (QCDA 2008). Projects involving visiting musicians obviously fulfil this brief well.

Types of engagement with musicians

By using the full range of musicians outlined above, a broad range of opportunities can be developed. We have seen a huge range of different projects ranging from sixth-form bands supporting 'Musical Futures' activities with younger students to long-term residencies with professional orchestras and opera companies.

There are basically three different types of engagement with musicians that could be provided for students, with many different permutations.

1. *Watching musicians at work*. Students could attend a rehearsal for a performance, or a composer could model how they generate ideas to meet a brief. This type of activity develops the students' understanding of creative processes and they gain insight into the music industry and musicians' working practices. This can have a profound effect on students' own creative work. For example, they might develop a deeper understanding of how composers continually refine their own work or how and where composers get their inspiration from. When composing themselves, they become eager to explore a range of stimuli and are more willing to refine and develop their original ideas.
2. *Attending a performance*. A concert brings the excitement of live music to the school or alternatively students may have the opportunity to visit a specialist venue. Some students may never have this experience other than as part of the music curriculum. This draws on the musicians' expertise as performers and the students appreciate (perhaps for the first time) high-quality work which can be truly inspirational for them.
3. *Working alongside musicians.* Students can work with a composer or performers to develop music together. This gives students opportunities for practical engagement in creative processes. They may be introduced to fresh techniques and ideas which develop their skills and musical understanding, and they are provided with access to new role models and ways of working which they can use afterwards in their own creative work.

Successful projects often include aspects all three, if not with the musicians themselves, then before and afterwards as the teacher sets the experience in context.

In one school, opportunities for students to learn a range of Indian instruments were already provided and there were a number of active ensembles in the school. Contact with the organisation which provided these lessons gave the school an opportunity to host a residency with visiting musicians from India. During the project, the musicians gave a series of performances on the sarod and tabla for different music classes, giving the students opportunities to listen and to ask questions. The teacher and the musicians helped the students to develop simple accompaniment parts on classroom instruments while the musicians improvised over the top. More confident students took turns at improvising as well, encouraged by the musicians. During the project, the musicians also worked with instrumentalists to compose a fusion piece involving a range of Western and Indian instruments. The students performed the piece with the musicians in an end-of-project concert for parents and children from a local primary school.

Benefits for students

Projects with musicians have the potential to inspire committed students by giving them access to high-quality musical experiences. It is also possible to engage other students by following their interests, and perhaps developing a project in a style that is really relevant to them. Visiting artists can develop a less formal relationship with students and some will respond well to this. Above all, the experience should enhance the curriculum and broaden students' experience of music-making.

Benefits for teachers

Working with other musicians has potential benefits for teachers as well as students. We have already suggested that teachers may learn new skills alongside students that can feed into curriculum development. The project may provide opportunities for teachers to observe students working with musicians, giving new insights into their potential and achievement. There is also the potential for raising the status of music as the students actively engage with and perform their work in the school and possibly beyond.

Benefits for musicians

Working on school-based projects gives musicians opportunities to share their expertise and skills with students and build relationships with potential audiences. Working with students can stimulate their own creativity and develop a different perspective of their work. Musicians develop their facilitation skills and their understanding of the school environment as well as issues such as inclusion.

Benefits for schools

Projects with musicians can often bring lasting benefits in school. For example, after the case study project described above, there was a renewed interest in Indian music in the school with an increased demand for instrumental lessons. Students who were learning these instruments already were much more willing to bring them to music lessons and use them as part of classroom ensembles. Some older students also set up an Indian dance club teaching younger students who then performed regularly with the Indian music ensembles in school concerts. There was evidence of impact on community cohesion within the school and on developing students' cultural understanding.

Impact is enhanced when the project is developed as an integral part of the music curriculum, rather than a 'one-off 'event which is intended as a good experience for students. As part of a unit of work, students get the most benefit from the experience in terms of developing their musical understanding. In the following case study, students watched a live performance during a unit of work on the Holocaust.

Teachers in History, RE and Music developed a cross-curricular project on the Holocaust for Year 9 students. The unit of work was designed to allow each subject to bring different and complementary dimensions to students' learning based around the key question: 'How should the Holocaust be remembered in Yorkshire?' The outcome of the unit was an individual or team project reflecting the key question and demonstrating the students' understanding. Ideas suggested included: a textbook 'double spread' appropriate for students a year younger; a song suitable for an act of remembrance; a recorded radio documentary on the experience of a local survivor; a presentation suitable for Holocaust Memorial Day (27 January) in an assembly; a documentary film using Moviemaker, including pictures and music; a small exhibition appropriate for a museum or gallery.

The unit of work was based around four themes: Pre-War Jewish Life, The Experience of Persecution, Lives in the Holocaust, and Beyond the Holocaust. In Music, students explored the impact of German propaganda on Jewish musicians and the music considered to be 'degenerate'; they experimented with a range of compositional techniques used in twentieth-century music, particularly exploring different starting points for composition such as tone rows, number sequences, graphics, visual art and 'chance' events. The focus for working with musicians in this unit was Steve Reich's 'Different Trains'. The students explored the compositional techniques used in the piece and were shown how Reich developed melodic phrases using text, some of it from Holocaust survivors. They were well prepared before they watched a live performance of the piece. Afterwards, students discussed the impact of the performance on their understanding of the Holocaust. They developed their own compositions in response to the writing and poems introduced in History and RE lessons. Later, in response to the key question 'How should the Holocaust be remembered in Yorkshire?' students discussed appropriate music for a memorial and developed a performance of a song focused on concepts of hope and remembrance.

Some projects have a more long-term impact on the music curriculum. In this case study, a school is working on a year-long residency project called PlayON with the Orchestra of Opera North. The following examples show how teachers are developing aspects of the music curriculum around activities supported by the orchestra.

In preparation for 'Meet the Orchestra Day', Year 7 students were introduced to orchestral instruments in a music lesson. All students in Year 7 attended a workshop with the orchestra and had the opportunity to play an orchestral instrument. Afterwards the unit of work focused on orchestral music.

Instrumentalists in the school have the opportunity to work more intensively with the orchestra in percussion and brass, string and woodwind ensembles. The workshops are supported by peripatetic teachers as much as possible in instrumental lessons. The school staff ensure that the ensembles continue to rehearse to maintain momentum and develop students' skills further.

A smaller group of Year 8 students have also taken part in a joint project focusing on *The Firebird* with Year 13 Art students, the artist Maria Hays and the composer Eve Harrison. A string trio from the orchestra performed for the Year 13 students and the students created multimedia art pieces in response to this. The Year 8 students took these and made them into a graphic score to tell a story and worked in their music lessons with the composer and members of the orchestra to develop a composition.

Organising a project

At this point, it is probably worth reiterating the National Curriculum guidance for working with a wide range of musicians; experiences do not necessarily have to be special projects with visiting professional musicians. Students can gain new insights by working with more experienced students in the school, with instrumental teachers and online opportunities for observing how musicians work. The following case study outlines how older students were used to support Musical Futures work with Year 9 students.

In one school, a Year 12 band was used to help a Year 9 class to develop instrumental skills on drum kit, bass, guitar and vocal skills. The class were split into four groups to learn the vocal and instrumental parts to Duffy's 'Mercy'. Using a carousel system, the students had the opportunity to learn all the parts before developing a class performance. The Year 9 students then worked on the Informal Learning activities outlined in the *Musical Futures Resource Pack* (2nd edn), and the Year 12 students dropped in every few lessons to support their work. When the students had reached the composing stage of the project, the Year 12 students led a workshop playing some of their own songs, explaining how they composed the music and answering students' questions, before spending some time supporting the Year 9 students in developing their own songs.

The following case studies outline how students can be given opportunities to engage with musicians using online tools.

In one school, students use Show Me How to Play (http://www.showmehowtoplay.com) to learn instrumental and vocal parts in pop songs. Using the Multiplayer, the students work in instrumental groups to learn their part and then mute it so that they can practise with the rest of the recorded band. Gradually students move into small ensemble groups to play all of the parts together.

Another music department uses Soundjunction (http://www.soundjunction.org) to give students the opportunity to engage with professional musicians, performers and composers, and to learn more about their work within the music industry. There are video resources where composers model composing processes, and interactive tools which enable students to try the techniques themselves.

Obviously when commissioning a project involving visiting musicians there are more things to consider and greater preparation will be needed. The initial step is to identify a clear purpose for the project and to consider how the experience will enhance existing provision and what the learning objectives and outcomes will be. A clear project brief at the outset can be used to present your case for funding, to show the intended benefits for students, staff and the school, and as the basis for a discussion with musicians and Arts organisations. How the project will be integrated into the music curriculum can be considered at this point. It is also important to consider how the project will contribute to the wider curriculum, for example by providing opportunities for developing personal, learning and thinking skills and students' understanding of the cross-curriculum dimensions. You may also consider whether this could be a cross curricular project and how you can involve as many students as possible. Clear aims and learning objectives from the outset will enable meaningful evaluation both during and after the project. A single person in the school should be identified to coordinate the project and liaise with all stakeholders.

The next step is to find the right partners to work with. Ofali (2004) suggests that musicians will need skills in presenting, the ability to build a rapport with students and staff, an awareness of the school environment, reliability and responsibility, and the ability to meet the inclusive agenda of the school. Operating fair recruitment practices, giving you the opportunity to consider a number of possible partners, is one way of ensuring the best provision. It is always advisable to interview before commissioning a musician or organisation. They should be able to provide you with references and evidence of previous work with young people. It is important always to follow these references up and of course to ensure that relevant Criminal Records Bureau (CRB) checks are in place.

The aims of the project need to be clear for all concerned and practical aspects such as timetabling arrangements, the space and equipment needed and outcomes such as performing opportunities need to be considered. It is important to define the teacher and musician roles carefully and to have an open discussion about the way in which students will engage with activities to ensure that everyone is clear about working practices. Involving and informing all staff is absolutely vital. These practical considerations can be a source of tension and a barrier to success if they have not been thought through properly at the planning stage. For example, who will supply the equipment? Who will be responsible for the setting up of instruments and equipment and clearing away afterwards? Who will be responsible for classroom management during the workshops? During the project it is important to allow some time for coordination in order to iron out any problems as they occur.

Afterwards, an evaluation of the project will involve making judgements about the quality and value of the experience against your stated aims and learning objectives. Sharing information with all stakeholders is important, and time for a final evaluation meeting should be built into the project. This will enable you to make decisions about future projects and develop best practice. You may consider how you can promote the benefits of the project and share the successes more widely across the school.

When scoping a project, funding is often the biggest concern. Musician's fees, travel and subsistence, materials and equipment, insurance, supply cover if needed, performance costs and sundries such as photocopying, refreshments, etc. will all need to be taken into account. Sources of funding for projects in school are available; for example, projects involving students working towards Arts Awards can apply to the Access Fund for help in funding workshops with visiting artists. The Arts Council England also has grant programmes. MusicLeader (http://www.musicleader.net) is a good source of information for other funding opportunities.

It is worth developing relationships with parent musicians, former students, local arts organisations, arts venues, universities and colleges to look for free sources of contact with musicians. Music degree and education programmes often need placements for students to develop projects in schools as part of their course.

At the end of their Post Graduate Certificate of Education (PGCE) course, university students worked collaboratively in small groups for a week in a number of local schools. Their brief was to design projects which would allow students to work with them as an ensemble. The students taught all year groups in their normal music lessons during the week, avoiding the need for timetable changes.

The projects were varied. Examples included: an African drumming workshop which started with the PGCE students playing as an ensemble, leading to the whole class performing the same piece with the students; a 'stomp' workshop in which students composed and choreographed their own pieces; and a PGCE student band which performed a number of contemporary pieces before leading the students through some songwriting techniques.

Key to the success of the project was the time made available to plan the sessions fully with music teachers in the weeks leading to the start of the event, ensuring that the work enhanced the units of work already being taught or acted as an introduction to work that continued after the students had gone. The PGCE students described the response to the projects as 'overwhelming' and the teachers particularly commented on the opportunities it gave for them to observe students working.

Some orchestras have truly inspiring projects with which young people of all musical backgrounds or none can be encouraged to participate. These often combine the use of digital technology with the best musicianship and with teacher guidance can really meet the performance needs of all students in the classroom.

One school took students to experience a digital residency by the Philharmonia Orchestra called 'Re-Rite'. This presents a digital video recording of Stravinsky's *The Rite of Spring* in which students move through different rooms to experience what it is like to be a member of different sections of the orchestra and to see and hear the music as they would during a performance. The installation also includes touch screen technology to control sounds as a virtual conductor, commentaries from performers and the conductor, and interaction with real performers and instruments. In particular, video cues help students to accurately play percussion parts on bass drum, tam-tam and others! This is a clear example of an externally available performance activity, which is accessible (using Guitar Hero style notation) and engaging for all students.

Local music services are also sources of projects which enable students to work with musicians.

In one local authority, the music service is offering secondary schools the opportunity to receive a five-week block of curriculum enhancement called 'Music Xtra' led by teams of staff with specialisms in keyboard, guitar, drumkit, vocals and music technology. Teams visit schools on Thursday mornings and teach the classes that are timetabled for music, bringing with them a range of instruments and equipment. The programme is designed to enhance existing units of work, giving students the chance to work on creative projects supported by professional musicians. The work is heavily subsidised by the music service, with schools contributing £150.

Summary

The new curriculum requires that students have the opportunity to work with a range of musicians. Using the whole range of opportunities available, including web-based resources, will make this financially viable. The benefits for students are clear: musicians can model creative processes and help them to develop a deeper understanding of conventions, processes and musical devices. Careful preparation and setting the visiting musician's work in context is important to maximise the impact of the experience and to enable students to incorporate ideas and processes learned into their own creative work. Evaluation afterwards ensures that projects undertaken add real value to the existing music curriculum. Finally, it is worth remembering that students already work with a musician in the classroom in every music lesson – you! If we model creative processes for the students and use every opportunity to play or sing for and with them, this will enhance the way they tackle their own projects and develop their musicianship and musical understanding.

Reflective Questions

1. Which units of work would benefit from engaging with musicians to further the students' understanding?
2. What opportunities are there to develop relationships with local organisations and musicians to initiate projects?
3. How can I increase my participation in lessons as a musician?

Further Reading

DfES (2006) *KS3 Music: A Professional Development Programme*, as revised DCSF (2008). Online at: http://www3.hants.gov.uk/music (accessed 28 November 2010). There are specific references to the role of musicians in the classroom in Unit 4: Modelling and in Unit 6: Feedback. Planning resources are available to support teachers in developing opportunities for students to work with musicians across the key stage.

Kenny, A. (2010) 'Too cool for school? Musicians as partners in education', *Irish Educational Studies*, 29(2): 153–66.

Woolfe, F. (2000) *From Policy to Partnership: Developing the Arts in Schools*. Arts Council England. Online at: http://www.artscouncil.org.uk/publication_archive/from-policy-to-partnership-developing-the-arts-in-schools/ (accessed 28 November 2010).

Zeserson, K. (2009) 'Musical collaborations with other adults', in J. Evans, and C. Philpott (eds), *A Practical Guide to Teaching Music in the Secondary School*. London: Routledge.

References

D'Amore, A. (2010) *Musical Futures: An Approach to Teaching and Learning* (2nd edn). Online at: http://www.musicalfutures.org.uk/resource/27389 (accessed 29 November 2010).

Ofali, A. (2004) *Artists Working in Partnerships with Schools*. Arts Council England. Online at: http://www.artscouncil.org.uk/publication_archive/artists-working-in-partnership-with-schools/ (accessed 28 November 2010).

Qualifications and Curriculum Authority (2007) *Music: Programme of Study for Key Stage 3 and Attainment Target*. London: QCA.

Qualifications and Curriculum Development Agency (2008) *Compelling Learning Experiences*. Online at: http://curriculum.qcda.gov.uk/key-stages-3-and-4/designing-your-curriculum/Design-activities/Compelling-learning-experiences/index.aspx (accessed 28 November 2010).

Websites

http://www.artsaward.org.uk (accessed 28 November 2010).
http://www.artscouncil.org.uk (accessed 28 November 2010).
http://www.musicleader.net (accessed 28 November 2010).
http://www.showmehowtoplay.com (accessed 28 November 2010).
http://www.soundjunction.org (accessed 28 November 2010).

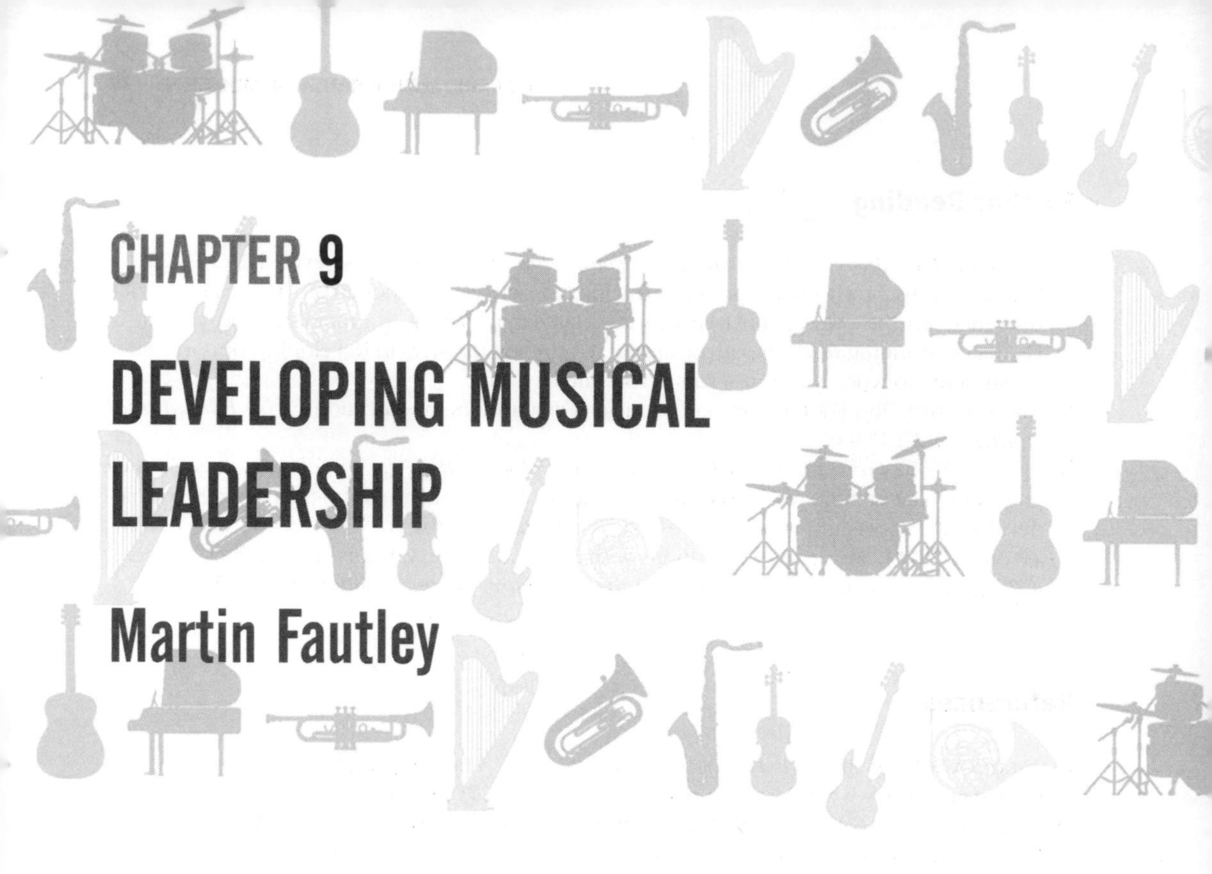

CHAPTER 9

DEVELOPING MUSICAL LEADERSHIP

Martin Fautley

Introduction

The notion of musical leadership, like many others in current educational discourse, is a contested one. The stance adopted in this chapter is that musical leadership allows students to become increasingly autonomous in their own music-making, becoming more able to make informed decisions about the sorts of music in which they wish to be involved, and helping them develop their own autonomous music-making and creating skills.

Musical leadership in the curriculum

The work of 'Musical Futures' (http://www.musicalfutures.org) has demonstrated that Key Stage 3 students are able to work autonomously at developing their own musical learning. Musical Futures was developed by Lucy Green, arising in part out of her research into the ways in which popular musicians learn (Green 2002):

> ... the aims of the project were to adopt and adapt aspects of popular musicians' informal music learning practices for use within the formal arena of the school classroom ... Each of the project's seven stages placed at its centre two or more of the five characteristics of informal learning ... These were: using music that pupils choose, like and identify with; learning by listening and copying recordings; learning with friends; engaging in personal, often haphazard learning without structured guidance, and integrating listening, performing, improvising and composing in all aspects of the learning process. (Green 2008b: 23)

What this means in terms of what is taking place in the classroom is that:

> Informal learning principles, drawn from the real-life learning practices and processes of popular musicians, are integrated into classroom work – enabling students to learn alongside friends, through independent, self-directed learning. Teachers take on different roles in this environment by acting as facilitators and musical models, rather than directors, and spend time standing back, observing and assessing the needs of their students, offering help, support and guidance based on objectives that students set for themselves. (Hallam et al. 2008: 10)

Working in this fashion, the students are engaged to a considerable extent in group work. The process of group dynamics in the classroom has been investigated over a number of years (Kutnick et al. 2005; Kutnick and Rogers 1984), and we know that one of the issues which arises is that of the dynamic of the group. In 'Musical Futures' work this led to an observation that leadership was one facet of this group work:

> Both group learning and peer-directed learning involved, in most groups, an amount of leadership by one or more members of the group. One interesting issue was that teachers expressed surprise about the extent to which leaders emerged in many groups. (Green 2008a: 184)

This notion of group work, and of the autonomy of the individual, is by no means confined solely to the work of 'Musical Futures'. After all, as the National Curriculum Importance Statement observes:

> Music education encourages active involvement in different forms of music-making, both individual and communal, helping to develop a sense of group identity and togetherness. Music can influence students' development in and out of school by fostering personal development and maturity, creating a sense of achievement and self-worth, and increasing students' ability to work with others in a group context. (QCA 2007: 179)

This Importance Statement takes us to the heart of the notion of musical leadership by students. This is the point made in the Curriculum Opportunities section of the National Curriculum, where it observes that students will 'build on their own interests and skills, taking on different roles and responsibilities and developing music leadership skills' (QCA 2007: 184). Not only does it act as a developmental modality, but it encourages 'self-worth' alongside cooperation skills. To this extent, it could be argued that aspects of musical leadership in students have a political dimension, a position adopted by the American music educator Paul Woodford:

> Music education is thus inevitably political and, owing to its potential for either promoting personal and collective freedom and growth or contributing to the musical disenfranchisement of children ... (by rendering them intellectually passive), it is something that should profoundly matter to society. (Woodford 2005: 31)

Learning and teaching principles and approaches

Affording leadership opportunities to students in music lessons does not involve abdicating all responsibility for content and structure to the students. Finney and Tymockzo (2003) describe five ways in which students can become enfranchised in music lessons by being offered some form of leadership role. These are:

- when they are selected to model appropriate musical behaviour, demonstrating and leading others by example;
- when they are invited to make positive contributions to planning and practice, offering their insights and analysis of teaching and learning to individual teachers in the process of learning;
- when, as older and more experienced students, they take the role of teacher's apprentice to support well-defined learning tasks;
- when they take on the role of researcher into some aspect of teaching and learning in music on behalf of their peers and in collaboration with their teacher;
- when students with out-of-school musical skill and expertise, unrecognised in school, are given opportunities for positive curriculum leadership with peers within school and in ways that will be of benefit to other students.

(Adapted from Finney and Tymoczko 2004)

The implications and principles of these ideas applied to the music class require some degree of unpicking in order to ascertain how they might be employed in the Key Stage 3 classroom. The National Curriculum for music can be viewed as a document of principles rather than of delineation of content. Thus, as we have seen in earlier chapters, music is organised through a series of 'Key Concepts' and 'Key Processes', in which specific musical examples are conspicuous by their absence. The 'explanatory notes' do list a range of styles, types, genres and musical components, but no specific *pieces* of music are mentioned. What this means is that learning is outlined, but the content specificity of the curriculum is left up to individual teachers in schools to make decisions in ways which will be most appropriate to their own and their students' needs.

Two separations

From the perspective of developing students as music leaders, this devolved decision-making is important as one of the key requirements of the National Curriculum is for music teachers to separate concepts of *doing* from those of *learning*. This is because the National Curriculum asks music teachers to consider the nature of what it is the students will be learning, and then to find appropriate means for this learning to be enacted in the classroom. One of the implications of this is that there needs to be a further separation, this time between *what* is to be learned and *how* it is to be learned. This can require some re-engineering of your mindset! To uncover what is involved in these two separations, let us consider what is involved in planning for musical learning and the role of students as musical leaders within this.

The traditional role of the teacher has been to plan for intended learning outcomes, the *what* is to be learned, and, simultaneously, to plan for content, the *how* it is to be learned. In many cases there has been a symbiotic relationship between the two. It was not that long ago that published materials for music education could be found which were essentially collections of activities. These fitted the 'doing' component of music lessons; the learning which was achieved by undertaking these activities was not always articulated. (Indeed, the very notion of separating learning from doing is one which is often quite complex anyhow.) In the light of this, separating the *what* of music learning from the *how* is an equally complex undertaking.

One of the first steps to be taken along this route is that of teachers reviewing their teaching and learning programmes for Key Stage 3. To be done effectively this should involve a 'root and branch' revision of the curriculum. Using the National Curriculum for guidance, and bearing in mind the specific nature of the location of the school setting, the music staff in the school need to ask themselves a number of key planning questions. A good place to start this process is in the Secondary Strategy units for professional development in music, especially the diagrammatic model of musical understanding (see Figure 9.1). This model delineates musical learning which leads towards musical understanding. It also highlights an area where students as musical leaders have the potential to shine, namely the acquisition and development of musical skills (see Figure 9.2).

The issue of skills is a thorny one! For example, some teachers value highly the skill of reading staff notation. On the other hand, this may not be a priority for some forms of musical endeavour with which the students are familiar. For

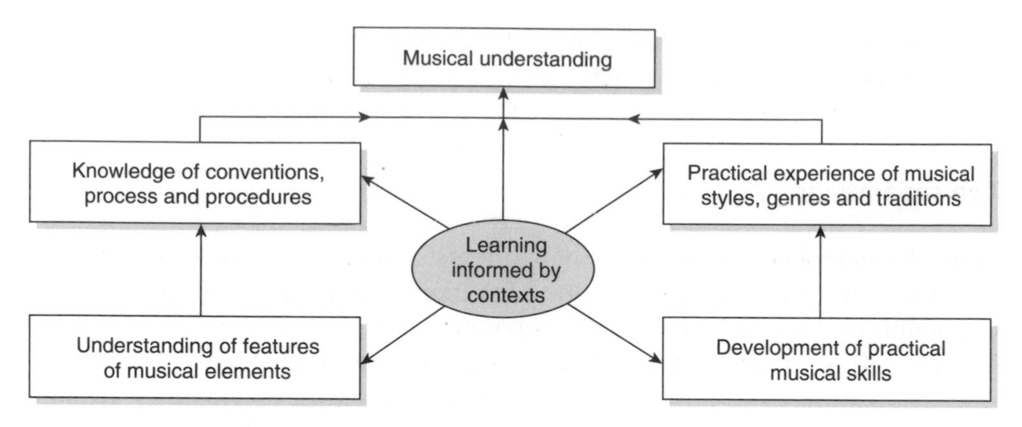

Figure 9.1 Model of musical understanding

Source: DfES (2006: 6).

Questions for teachers

(A) Teacher values:

What aspects of musical skill do you value most in your students?
What does your curriculum do to foster the skills you value?
Are there aspects of musical skill which you do not value?
Does your curriculum do anything to devalue these skills?

(B) Pupil values:

What aspects of music skill do your students value most?
What does your curriculum do to foster the skills the students value?
Are there skills which the students value which your curriculum does not?
Does this matter?

Figure 9.2 Key questions for teachers

example, a highly accomplished dhol drum ensemble may not need to read staff notation (nor might there be much music for them if they could!). But does that mean that these expert young musicians do not have anything to offer? The process of valuing some skills over others may be tacit; in other words, it may be that undervaluing takes place by omission. Key Stage 3 music is broad in scope, and the omission of things is an inevitable corollary to there being too much to do and too little time in which to do it.

The notion of prioritisation of content is one which all teachers will have to deal with. Historically, many KS3 syllabi represent a musical tour through a range of styles, types and genres: Gamelan, Samba, Blues, Waltzes, Theme and Variations, Ragas, Programme Music, African Drumming and so on. Teachers have taken these and placed them sequentially so that learning occurs through contact with these musics. In the course of the programme, skills, knowledge and understanding arise. When done well, these curricula are aimed, as Kevin Rogers puts it, at students 'developing cultural understanding, not just cultural exposure' (2009: 13). Done badly they can just be a 'Cook's Tour' of music. But the point is that the teacher has had to decide *what* to include. To put in Blues, they have had to leave out Samba (or whatever), to keep Gamelan, they have not got time for Raga. These, and similar decisions, bearing in mind Ofsted's injunction to 'do more of less' (2009: 14) place an enormous pressure on the curriculum. By using the starting point of the students' own interests and utilising the skills and enthusiasms of young musical leaders, ways can be found to deal with this, by starting from these and then moving beyond them.

One of the key changes between iterations of the National Curriculum has been the shift in language from the imperative of teaching to that of learning. In the former the phraseology was 'students should be taught how to ...'; in the latter the usage is 'students should be able to ...'. This is a significant shift away from a command-style delivery of music lessons towards one where the emphasis is on the students. What this means is that it is no longer enough for teaching to have taken place, the emphasis is now on learning.

Portrait of a young musical leader

Gary was a quiet, unassuming boy from whom his teachers generally reported average results. Early on in music lessons he asked if he could work on a computer with headphones on a song he been working on at home. It transpired that he had a major interest in composing and mixing his own music in electronic dance styles. His teacher recognised this potential and reordered the teaching and learning programme so that Gary could not only work on his own music, but could share his knowledge with others. Gary became looked up to by the others as a key source of musical knowledge. He went on to use his skills to undertake some developed compositional activities.

The change of emphasis from teaching to learning also marks a shift in accountability and in classroom dynamics. With this shift we are looking to the students to be much more agentive in their own learning. This takes us back to the notion of student-valorised skills, and in many ways this has resonances with the last of the bullet points from Finney and Tymockzo cited earlier. Skills evidenced and valued by the students do not need to be inimical to those of National Curriculum music. Indeed, the advice of Mrs Curwen's 1886 piano method 'Proceed from the known to the related unknown' (Curwen 1886) is apposite here and still relevant today. The students know what they know and tend to like what they know. The job of the teacher is to take them to the 'related unknown'. In many cases, these will be 'unknown unknowns', as the students will not be aware of what they don't know. Skill acquisition, therefore, can proceed from those things which musical leaders are able to do and help with towards those things which they do not know about. This is an area where involving students as musical leaders can have significant impact. As Finney and Tymockzo observe:

> They want learning to be collaborative and to engage with what is prevalent now in their imaginations. Young adolescents are active and competent members of society. They are much more than passive subjects of social structures. (Finney and Tymockzo 2004)

This may seem a long way from a discussion concerning skill acquisition, but the key question to ask is that suggested in this last quotation: young people want to '...engage with what is prevalent now in their imaginations'. This means making the curriculum relevant to the students.

The notion of curricular relevance takes us back to the notion of separating the *what* of musical learning from the *how*. There is some inevitability about the planning of a curriculum for the whole of a key stage, the *what*, which the music department in a school will want to have control over, but within this there are issues about students as musical leaders having responsibility over the *how*. What this involves could be referred to as *distributed leadership* (Price 2005: 5), where the decision-making is spread between students and teacher. As we saw earlier, doing this does not necessarily involve handing all decisions about learning to the students, a thought which many will find uncomfortable. What it can mean, however, is involving the students in decision-making about their own learning. This can also be a way of addressing the issue of personalising the curriculum. Where students have a stake in the direction of their own musical pathway, they are more likely to be engaged, as this music teacher observed:

> ... the key thing for me is that where before students always felt that they had to jump through the hoops put out by the teacher, in Musical Futures the students revel in setting their own targets. Once they feel they are making decisions for themselves, there is no stopping them ... (Price and D'Amore 2007: 5)

This takes us back to Mrs Curwen again, as the music teacher will have an overall view as to how to proceed through the Key Stage, and how to move from the 'known to the related unknown', the young musical leaders will provide help and support in navigating the path through this, starting from what they know.

Musical leaders and learning

So, what is there to learn in music education, and what are the roles of musical leadership in this? What do the students want to learn? What do you want them to learn? These are more difficult questions! According to the National Curriculum there are the Key Concepts: the integration of practice between performing, composing and listening; cultural understanding; critical understanding; creativity; and communication; and the Key Processes of performing, composing, and listening; reviewing and evaluating; all delivered through a range of contexts within and beyond the classroom. We also know that curriculum opportunities should exist for students to develop a range of individual skills in performing, composing and listening, and to develop their music leadership skills too.

A wide range of skills are involved in music-making and learning at Key Stage 3 which young musical leaders might possess to differing degrees. The list shown in Figure 9.3 provides just a small sample of these.

An interesting exercise for teachers revising their Key Stage 3 programmes of study would be to see how many skills from Figure 9.3 are included in their own intended learning outcomes, and to add to this the skills which are not on the list which will also be covered.

Skills:

DJ'ing	Playing scales	Sampling
Beatboxing	Playing chords	Composing using ICT
Mixing	Singing	Multitrack recording
Rapping	Singing harmonies	Ringtone composing
MC'ing	Improvising	Melody writing
Playing by ear	Songwriting	Playing a solo

Figure 9.3 Some Key Stage 3 Music Leader skills

From skills to understanding

Although music education involving young people as music leaders involves a considerable emphasis upon skills and skill acquisition, as we argued in Chapter 2, the goal is to aim for musical understanding. It is possible to construct an entire music education based solely on learning skills – indeed, many of the worst examples of instrument teaching fall into this trap – but a true musical *education* aims for understanding, not mere regurgitation; this is the difference between learning and instruction. To do this, the National Curriculum recognises that the purpose of music learning is to integrate performing, composing and listening, and to do so in a *musical* fashion.

Young musical leaders have a role to play here too. The comfort zone of their own ability, while a source of strength, will also need developing. Take the case of the young dhol drummers mentioned above. They are able to perform to a very high standard, and their achievements in dhol drumming are contextually specific and highly developed. But in order for them to progress they need to be taken on a journey too. For them, one place to start might be for them to compose their own rhythms. They can broaden their repertoire by coming up with new variants on pieces they can play already. They can be teamed with other instrumentalists so that they form the rhythmic backing while other melodic and harmonic work takes place alongside them. All of these activities are undertaken with a view to developing their musical understanding, the key factor in all of this.

It is very difficult to know what it means to understand an aspect of music. While there clearly needs to be a basic skill set in order for students to be able to make up their own music, the question becomes how basic does this skill set have to be? Knowing that at Key Stage 3 most composing is undertaken directly on the instruments concerned, how little is enough, in terms of what is needed to begin to compose or perform? Do classroom instruments offer the potential for this in a way which is manageable?

The role of ICT, and the story of Gary above, tell us that what we might think is enough might be more than sufficient. Gary's story has many resonances with those of Dizzy Rascal, the rapper and songwriter, who observed that the music department at his school '... was the only place in school that I actually wanted to be' (*Observer* 2003). It can also be the case that young musical leaders like Gary are able to build on their skills and exploit them in a way which enables them to use them in the service of producing new music, as well as in recreating extant works. This is another role for musical leaders and, again, involves stretching them.

Summary

This chapter has looked at the role that young music leaders have to play in the development of teaching and learning activities during Key Stage 3. It has done this by considering the ways in which young people can have an input into the types of activity which take place in the music class at this stage and has discussed how these can be best integrated. This continues the theme of empowering learners discussed in Chapter 4. One of the key messages has been that music education should not simply be the handing down of an accepted skill set from one group of people to another, but that skills form only part of the education of a well-rounded musician. The opportunities afforded by the National Curriculum for music should mean that teachers and learners are in a better position to consider what the young people at their school bring with them to music learning and to capitalise upon this accordingly. The notion of 'distributed leadership' should be something that music teachers, may be more than those of other subjects, are aware of and comfortable with. This will certainly be the case in extra-curricular music-making activities, where it seems unlikely that a teacher will be able to play all of the instruments in an ensemble. Transferring this to the classroom should be a relatively straightforward step for the teacher to take.

One of the effects of involving the notion of musical leadership in Key Stage 3 teaching and learning is that the curriculum is unlikely to become ossified. The set of skills shown in Figure 6.3 represents just a small number of what could be found among Key Stage 3 students. Each new year will bring new additions to the skill set and will involve new challenges. Involving these young musical leaders will go a long way towards the personalisation of the curriculum to meet the needs of the learners!

Reflective Questions

1. What does the Key Stage 3 curriculum require in terms of skills, knowledge and understanding? Why are these included? What justifications can I give?
2. Do the students in my school have any ownership of the skills they want to develop?
3. How reactive is the Key Stage 3 programme of study? Is it the same each year?
4. How much involvement do students have in the path of their own learning? How much ownership do the students have over the content of music lessons? In what ways could students be involved in plotting their own musical pathways?

Further Reading

DfES (2006) 'Unit 1: Structuring Learning for Musical Understanding', *KS3 Music: A Professional Development Programme*, as revised. Online at: http://www.ks3music.org.uk (accessed 21 November 2010).

Finney, J. and Tymockzo, M. (2003) 'Students as leaders in music: the potential for music education', *Music Education International*, 2(1): 25–41.

Green, L. (2008) *Music, Informal Learning and the School: A New Classroom Pedagogy*. Aldershot: Ashgate.

Price, D. (2005) *Transforming Musical Leadership*. London: Paul Hamlyn.

References

Curwen, A. J. (1886) *The Teacher's Guide to Mrs. Curwen's Pianoforte Method (the child pianist). Being a practical course in the elements of music*. London: Curwen's Edition.

DfES (2006) 'Unit 1: Structuring Learning for Musical Understanding', *KS3 Music: A Professional Development Programme, as revised*. Online at: http://www.ks3music.org.uk (accessed 21 November 2010).

Finney, J. and Tymockzo, M. (2003) 'Students as leaders in music: the potential for music education', *Music Education International*, 2(1): 25–41.

Goehr, L. (1992) *The Imaginary Museum of Musical Works*. Oxford: Clarendon Press.

Green, L. (2002) *How Popular Musicians Learn: A Way Ahead for Music Education*. London and New York: Ashgate.

Green, L. (2008a) 'Group cooperation, inclusion and disaffected students: some responses to informal learning in the music classroom', *Music Education Research,* 10 (2): 177–92.

Green, L. (2008b) *Music, Informal Learning and the School: A New Classroom Pedagogy*. Aldershot: Ashgate.

Hallam, S., Creech, A., Sandford, C., Rinta, T. and Shave, K. (2008) *Survey of Musical Futures for the Paul Hamlyn Foundation*. London: Institute of Education.

Hymas, C. (1991) 'The Great Composers expelled from school', *Sunday Times,* 7 July.

Kutnick, P. and Rogers, C. (1984) 'Groups in classrooms', in P. Kutnick and C. Rogers (eds), *Groups in Schools*. London: Cassell.

Kutnick, P., Blatchford, P. and Baines, E. (2005) 'Grouping of pupils in secondary school classrooms: possible links between pedagogy and learning', *Social Psychology of Education,* 8(4): 349–74.

Observer (2003) Online at: http://observer.guardian.co.uk/omm/story/0,,1043910,00.html (accessed 1 October 2010).

Ofsted (2009) *Making More of Music*. London: Ofsted.

Pitts, S. (2000) *A Century of Change in Music Education*. Aldershot: Ashgate.

Price, D. (2005) *Transforming Musical Leadership*. London: Paul Hamlyn Foundation.

Price, D. and D'Amore, A. (2007) *From Vision to Practice – A Summary of Key Findings*. London: Paul Hamlyn Foundation.

Qualifications and Curriculum Authority (2007) *Music: Programme of Study for Key Stage 3 and Attainment Target*. London: QCA.

Rogers, K. (2009) 'Musical Progress: "it depends what you mean by ..."', in H. Coll and A. Lamont (eds), *Exploring Musical Development.* Matlock: NAME.

Swanwick, K. (1979) *A Basis for Music Education*. Windsor: NFER-Nelson.

Woodford, P. (2005) *Democracy and Music Education: Liberalism, Ethics, and the Politics of Practice*. Bloomington, IN: Indiana University Press.

PART 3

ENRICHING MUSICAL MODELS OF DEVELOPMENT AND ASSESSMENT

The final section of the book explores two issues of significant importance to music teachers: musical development and assessment. While chapters 10 and 11 focus particularly on Key Stage 3, the final chapter outlines approaches to teaching the 14–19 curriculum which focus on developing students as independent learners, ready to take ownership of their music making.

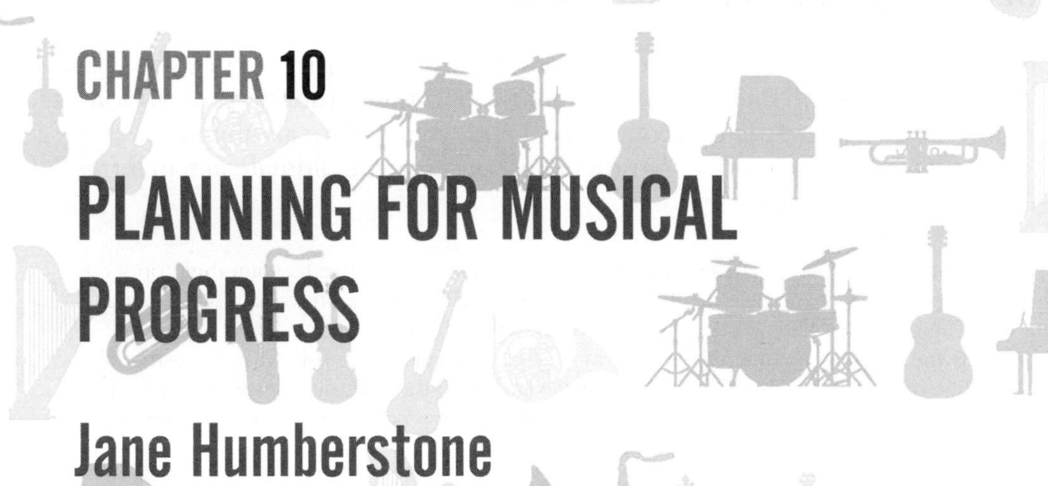

CHAPTER 10

PLANNING FOR MUSICAL PROGRESS

Jane Humberstone

Introduction

The concepts explored in the previous chapters of the book already have significant implications for how you might plan a music curriculum. We have argued for:

- an integrated approach to the Key Concepts and Processes and the inclusion of approaches such as cross-curricularity, PLTS and Functional Skills;
- making connections with the wider world of musicians and music in society;
- developing new approaches for using music technology;
- giving students more ownership of the content of their curriculum and the way in which they learn.

In this final section of the book, we consider curriculum planning and assessment in Key Stage 3 in more detail. This chapter will look at how you can develop a long-term plan which supports the development of your students' musical understanding in a coherent way. It does this through a simple, two-stage model built around the concepts of a curriculum map overview and a map for developing individual units of work.

Developing musical understanding

Before we can begin to plan the scheme of work for music, we need to consider a definition of 'understanding' in music and the nature of 'progression': what it means to get better in our subject and what we are aiming for.

Swanwick (1979) describes 'aesthetic response' as the ultimate aim in terms of students' outcomes.

> An aesthetic response is self-enriching ... It is basically a response to something on its own terms and for the sake of what it means for us; a flower or a firework, a picture or a pop-song, an evocative word, or the whole new world of a book. An aesthetic experience feeds the imagination and affects the way we feel about things; music without aesthetic qualities is like a fire without heat. We acknowledge the aesthetic qualities every time we say things like 'He has a good technique but his playing seems so insensitive and unmusical'. Skills alone are not enough. (Swanwick 1979: 60–1)

Swanwick (1979, 1999) goes on to identify five parameters of musical experience which should shape the music curriculum:

- *Composition* in its broadest sense – all forms of musical invention.
- *Literature Studies* – knowledge about music and musicians, e.g. theoretical understanding, knowledge about composers, understanding musical terms, etc.
- *Audition or Audience Listening* – more than listening to a recorded or live piece of music but the listening required when playing in an ensemble and making creative decisions when composing, improvising, etc. Swanwick (1979: 43) describes this as: '... attending to the presentation of the music as an audience. It is a very special form of mind often involving empathy with the performers, a sense of musical style relevant to the occasion, a willingness to "go along with" the music and ultimately an ability to respond to the musical object as an aesthetic entity.'
- *Skill Acquisition* – developing aural, instrumental and notational skills.
- *Performance* – making music together and communicating with an audience.

Swanwick describes Composition, Audition and Performance as category I objectives, and Literacy and Skill Acquisition as category II objectives, acknowledging that the category II objectives are only instrumental to achieving category I objectives.

Philpott (2007) describes different aspects of musical knowledge as:

- knowledge 'about' music, focusing on factual knowledge, knowledge about composers, style, theory and musical concepts;

- 'how to' knowledge, focusing on technical skills, aural discrimination, presentational skills, an understanding of notation and the 'craft' of being able to make music sound a particular way;
- knowledge 'of' music, focusing on the aesthetic response, understanding the expressive potential of music and developing an emotional attachment and relationship with music.

Philpott also outlines the hierarchical relationship between these different forms of musical knowledge: the 'how to' and the knowledge 'about' music enhances students' knowledge 'of' music.

As outlined in the previous chapter, the National Strategy KS3 Music Professional Development Programme (DfES 2006a) develops a comprehensive model of musical understanding arising from:

- learning about musical conventions, processes and devices and the way that musical elements are used to create intended effects;
- the development of students' practical skills together with varied experience of different musical styles, genres and traditions (see Figure 9.1).

Again, there is the concept of musical understanding being a higher goal, demonstrated by musicianship, musicality and aesthetic awareness.

These concepts of musical understanding have clear implications for planning the music curriculum. Firstly, theoretical, historical and notational knowledge aids musical understanding but should be embedded in activities where students explore these practically as musicians. Secondly, students need to explore a wide range of styles, genres and traditions across time and place and, finally, emphasis should be placed on the 'quality' of musical responses and outcomes.

Musical progress

In the National Curriculum, emphasis on developing students' understanding of the contexts of music studied is highlighted. The Importance Statement outlines music as 'an integral part of culture, past and present. Music helps pupils to understand themselves, relate to others and develop their cultural understanding' (QCA 2007a: 179). This is an important part of developing students' musical understanding, as they explore how contexts impact directly on the music and influence its aesthetic value. This increasing sense of musical style and intent, together with increasing confidence to be imaginative and creative, impacts enormously on the quality of students' musical responses and is one aspect that demonstrates musical progress.

The KS3 Strategy materials (DfES 2006a) outline two other aspects of musical progression: breadth and depth. Breadth is concerned with the range of musical experiences that students have across the curriculum. It is argued that styles, genres and traditions have distinctive modes of musical thinking which develop students' musical understanding. Styles (focusing on music across time and place) are defined by the consistent use of particular conventions, processes and devices which students will need to explore to develop their understanding. This represents a relatively 'directed or closed' form of musical learning.

Genres (music written for specific purposes) suggest a more 'guided' form of learning as some characteristics of the music will be fixed where as others can be varied. For example, wedding marches will all have the same 'processional' qualities but can use different musical resources depending on the context.

Traditions (ways of working or producing) suggest the most 'open' form of learning as the musical outcomes are more difficult to predict. Traditions cut across styles and genres. For example, you might decide to focus on improvisation as a musical tradition and explore how this is exploited in different kinds of music across time and place. The Strategy materials (DfES 2006a) suggest that in order to for students to experience all three types of musical thinking and learning, there should be a balance of units of work focusing on styles, genres and traditions across the curriculum.

In the National Curriculum programme of study, breadth is also outlined in the Range and Content and Curriculum Opportunities sections, for example: opportunities to work with a range of musicians; opportunities to work individually, in small groups and in class ensembles; opportunities to explore links between music and other areas of the curriculum; opportunities to take part in a range of performing activities both inside and outside of the classroom, etc. As students have these broad range of musical experiences in the curriculum, their confidence in musical thinking and responding grows, leading to increased musical understanding.

The final aspect of progression in music is depth. This is discussed initially in Chapter 2 in terms of increasing expectations in the Key Processes. The principles developed further here are rooted in the Secondary National Strategy (DfES 2006b). Within this model, the levels of attainment statements in the Key Stage 3 Programme of Study are aligned to six stages of musical progression. These stages outline the stages of progression in terms of depth of musical understanding. This evolves from recognising sound to discriminating expressive and interpretive features; from responding to sound to exploiting resources and challenging conventions. The adaptation shown in Table 10.1 shows the stages of progression for Levels 4–6.

Table 10.1 Stages of progression

Stage of progression	Objectives for understanding	Level outcomes
Identify and Manipulate	Learn how musical sounds can be manipulated into effective, predictable patterns and structures to reflect simple contexts by: Learning how to use patterns of sound to create a specific mood for a defined but basic expressive purpose	*Level 4*: Students identify and explore the relationship between sounds and how music reflects different intentions
Identify and Relate	Learn how musical styles, genres or traditions and the conventions they use can be compared and related to their origins by: Learning how to experiment with combinations of conventions to meet a range of expressive purposes that reflect changing contexts	*Level 5:* Students identify and explore musical devices and how music reflects time, place and culture
Identify and Integrate	Learn how details of musical conventions can be developed to express individual ideas, while staying integrated within a given style, genre or tradition by: Learning how to explore within a range of idiomatic musical styles, genres or traditions, integrating their own ideas into stylistically consistent outcomes	*Level 6:* Students identify and explore the different processes and contexts of selected musical styles, genres and traditions

Adapted from DfES (2006b).

When long-term planning, you will need to ensure that classroom activities throughout the Key Stage allow students to demonstrate work at the highest levels. Understanding the stages of progression embedded in the level descriptors are key to placing musical experiences at appropriate points in the long-term plan as well as making connections between units of work.

Placing units of work within the curriculum needs careful consideration. While different types of music are not intrinsically more difficult than any other, what will determine their order is the expectation in terms of developing students' musical understanding (DfES 2006a).

The latest revision of the National Curriculum has been designed to allow greater flexibility for schools to design and personalise their own curriculum.

> In particular, with less prescribed content teachers will be able to personalise the curriculum, designing learning experiences to meet individual needs and engage all learners. They will have the flexibility to provide focused support and greater challenge where needed, helping to ensure that all learners have the opportunity to make progress and achieve. (QCA 2007b: 4)

Although we have never had highly defined 'content' in the music curriculum, it is totally appropriate to consider at departmental level what sort of music curriculum is most appropriate for your particular students. This would be a logical starting point for revising the Key Stage 3 scheme of work. Including the views of students should be part of this early development.

In one school, the music department collected views from Year 8 students as part of their curriculum review. Views were collected across the year group using a focus group from each class. The students said that they really enjoyed working on steel pans more than other instruments; they enjoyed singing in lessons; they liked it when students who played instruments played them during class performing activities as it made the pieces sound better; they enjoyed passing on their skills to others, but only when the students were younger than them; they liked being videoed when performing and thought they learned most when they had the opportunity to watch it and then refine their work further. When they had completed a performing or composing project they wanted to write about it. They also had views about the sort of music they wanted to learn which included more pop music and learning to play the guitar and drums.

The music department concentrated staff development time on exploring their aims for the Key Stage 3 music curriculum. They discussed what they wanted students to know and be able to do and the characteristics of successful learners in music. Taking each of their characteristics in turn they highlighted them as: green – seen in the majority of learners (an area of strength); amber – seen in many learners but not particularly strong; and red – only seen in a few learners (an area for development). This led into further evaluation of existing units of work and the development of a new curriculum map for Key Stage 3 music.

The National Strategy KS3 Music Professional Development Programme (DfES 2006c) outlines the following aims of the Key Stage 3 curriculum which you might find useful.

To enable pupils to:

- Develop their understanding of a culturally diverse range of musical styles, genres and traditions.
- Understand how music reflects and is influenced by the contexts within which it is created, performed and listened to.
- Articulate verbally and practically the conventions, processes and devices of different musical styles, genres and traditions.
- Understand how the features of musical elements impact on music.
- Use relevant practical skills for music-making.
- Be inspired by vibrant and relevant music-making.

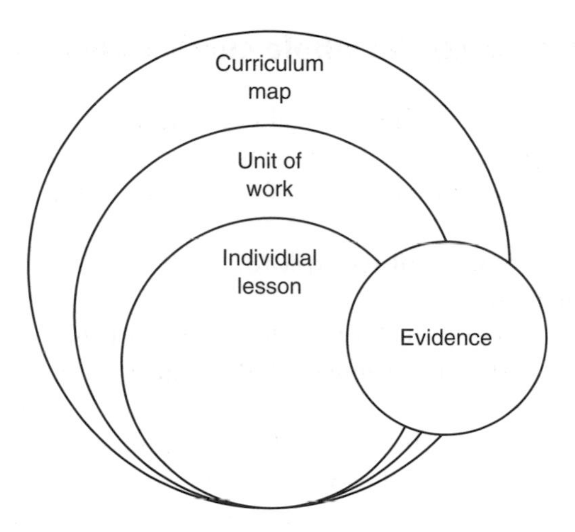

Figure 10.1 Long-, medium- and short-term planning

Curriculum planning

Our approach to planning for musical learning starts with a consideration of the whole music curriculum. This holistic approach acknowledges that a vibrant curriculum requires many different facets including different learning and teaching styles, different approaches, different experiences of musical styles, genres and traditions. Within this whole, each unit of work only serves as a minor part in pupils becoming skilful musicians, successful learners, confident individuals and responsible citizens.

Figure 10.1 shows the interrelationship of the whole curriculum 'map' and the shorter-term aspects of planning for a unit of work. The biggest circle is the foundation for all the other elements. Evidence-gathering needs to be considered at each stage as this is key to tracking students' progress.

Once the curriculum map is in place, each unit of work or 'topic' can be considered in more detail. Each topic needs to ensure that students' musical understanding is developed through the appropriate use of Key Concepts and Key Processes. During our time as subject advisors for the new curriculum, we used a simple planning tool to facilitate this process. Having used this tool, teachers were always impressed by the compelling learning experiences it generated for their students. This process is built around two stages:

- Developing the whole curriculum map
- Mapping the individual unit of work.

Stage One: Developing the whole curriculum map

The first stage is to identify the musical context and the learning context for each unit of work within your whole curriculum map. To do this, answer the following four questions for each unit of work you wish the students to study:

- What is the music you want to explore?
- What is this music for?
- What do you want your students to learn about this music?
- How will students develop their understanding of the music?

At this point in the process, there is likely to be a mixture of confident answers to these questions when considering existing units of work which you want to keep, and reasonably clear ideas about new units of work which you want to include to support specific developments in the music curriculum arising from your departmental discussions above.

The following five steps will help you to begin the process of placing units of work appropriately in the curriculum map overview (Figure 10.2).

Step 1

Put your answer to the question 'What is the music you want to explore?' in the 'Music Studied' boxes for as many of your areas of the map as possible. Next, add the answers to the second question 'What is this music for?' in the 'Purpose' boxes.

For example, if the music studied is 'gospel', its purpose could be 'songs for worship'; if the music focuses on ballads in folk music, the purpose may be to tell a story and/or politically influence people. These two questions are the most critical.

Step 2

The third question is 'What do you want your students to learn about this music?' In other words, what is the key learning that the unit will contain? In our gospel example this could be that gospel music derives from work song with influences from spirituals, hymns and jazz. These can be added to the curriculum map overview in the 'Key Learning' boxes.

Remind yourself of the stages of progression from the 'Defining Musical Understanding' document (DfES 2006b) and decide roughly where your chosen unit sits within this. For example, when composing a folk ballad, students may begin to 'break conventions' and may even 'explore the details of stylistic idioms, bringing some individuality to their work' in the 'Identify and

Year	Key Concepts	Term 1	Term 2	Term 3	Term 4	Term 5	Term 6
7	Music Studied						
	Purpose						
	Key Learning						
	How						
8	Music Studied						
	Purpose						
	Key Learning						
	How						
9	Music Studied						
	Purpose						
	Key Learning						
	How						

Key concepts:

1.2 Cultural Understanding

What is the music you want to explore? (Music studied) What is the music for? (Purpose)

1.3 Critical Understanding

What do you want the students to learn about this music? (Key Learning)

1.1 Integration of Practice

How will students develop their understanding of the music? (How)

1.4 Creativity

Where are the places we can develop creativity? Are there opportunities to work with other areas?

1.5 Communication

Are there areas to incorporate expression through music?

Figure 10.2 Curriculum map

Integrate' stage. This might suggest to you that the unit is best placed within Year 9. In the gospel example you may have decided that the students should be singing in this clearly defined style and will therefore be working within the 'Identify and Manipulate' stage, i.e. more suited to Year 7.

Position your units of work on the curriculum map overview in the best places in light of these considerations.

Step 3

The final question drawn from Figure 10.2 is 'How will students develop their understanding of the music?' This question starts to consider the Key Processes that the students will need to engage with in order to develop during each unit. For our gospel topic, students may learn primarily through performing songs, whereas in the folk unit they could learn primarily through composing songs. Add this to the 'How?' boxes in the curriculum map. Remember to keep it simple at this stage, i.e. the words 'performing' or 'composing' may be enough here.

Step 4

We can audit the curriculum map overview to ensure that we are developing a broad range of musical experiences for students. You could colour code the map to identify the different Key Processes being utilised, or the different types of music being studied (by genre, style or tradition), or the different types of learning the students might be engaged in (formal/informal, etc.).

Step 5

Stand back and have a look. Are there a variety of colours? If not, where would your students benefit from a different approach being taken? Is there a music/learning style which would lend itself naturally to this? Are there spaces on the map due to you not being able to answer the questions? If yes, reconsider what kind of opportunity for musical learning would fill the gap.

Stage Two: Mapping the individual unit of work

This second task helps to refine individual units of work within the curriculum map and to consider whether they are placed appropriately to facilitate and evidence musical understanding. To do this, select one of the Units of Work that you have included within your curriculum overview map (perhaps start with one of the topics for which the questions in Stage One were easiest to answer). Work through the following four steps.

Step 1

Use the Unit Map (Figure 10.3) to develop the unit of work further. The initial questions from the first exercise have been expanded to consider all five Key Concepts. Start with the questions from the previous exercise – the Key Concept of Cultural Understanding. This starting point ensures that students develop an awareness of the context of the music, the 'where', 'when', 'who' and 'why' of the music. This is always at the foundation of the planning process.

Step 2

Next expand on the Critical Understanding. This is where you will decide which conventions, processes and devices make the music unique and are essential for the students to learn. For example, in the Year 7 gospel unit you may extract syncopation, the use of major keys and the use of simple hymn-like harmonies. Ask yourself what sort of learning will the students be engaged in? Are there opportunities to link to other related music?

Step 3

You can now expand on the Key Concept of Integration of Practice. In Stage One, you identified broadly how the Key Processes might develop students' understanding of the topic. You can start to refine this by thinking about the activities that you will engage them in. For example, in our Year 9 folk ballad project, singing a meaningful ballad such as the *Dalesman's Litany*, using expressive vocal skills to convey the downtrodden feeling of those oppressed by the Industrial Revolution, could have a great influence on the students' individual, personal statements of their own social or political world view.

Step 4

Now consider the Key Concepts of Creativity and Communication. This is an opportunity to make the learning come alive. Can you make links to the real world or other curriculum areas? Are there ways to make the learning more compelling for the students?

At this point, you may want to go back to your curriculum map overview and add some additional details. Consider how the units link to each other and whether they are coherent in developing students' music understanding. You may need to develop specific units of work to fill any gaps in the curriculum map. The aim of this long-term planning is for the department to have a very clear understanding of how each unit of work supports the development of the next. You are now in a position to do a much more detailed audit:

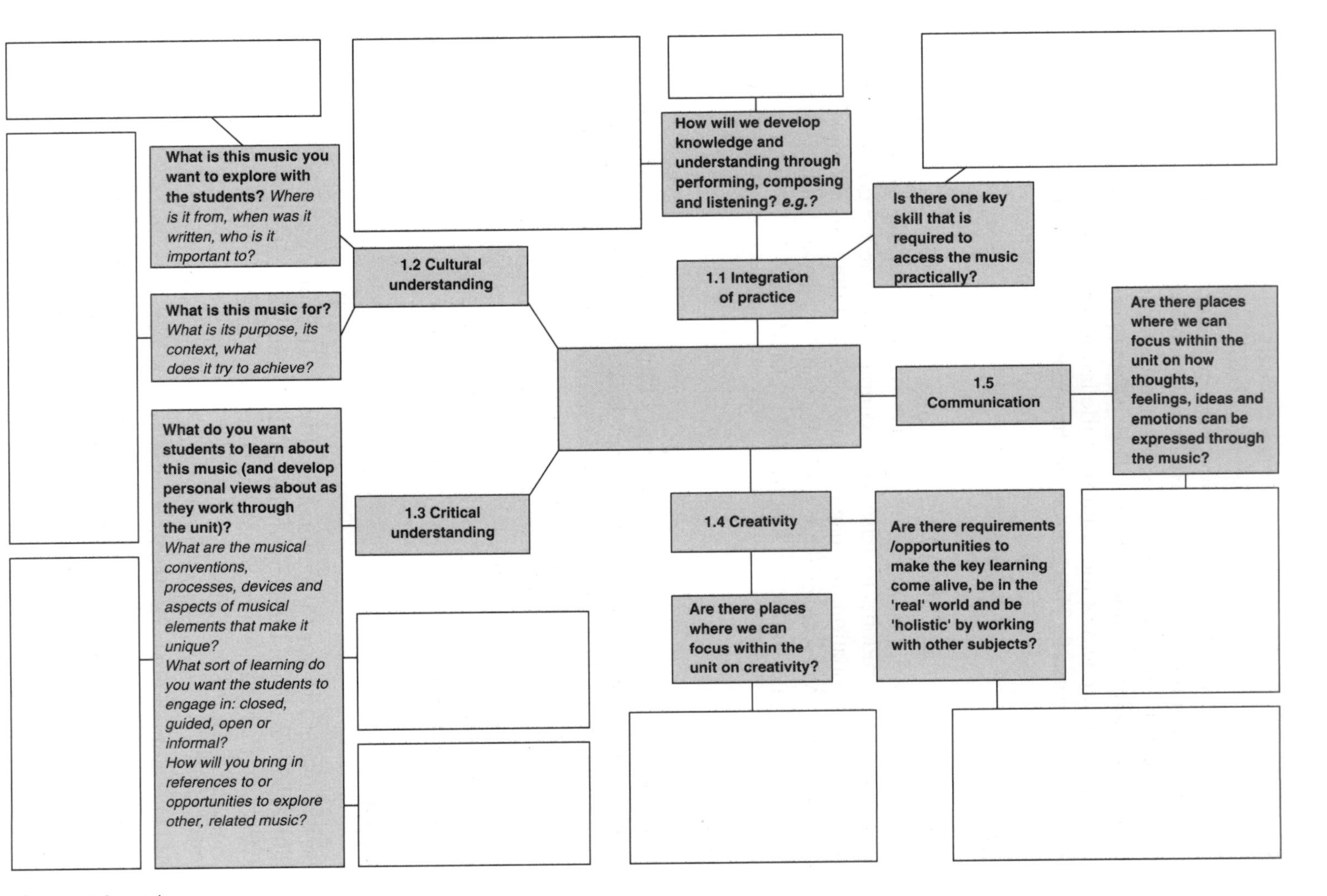

Figure 10.3 Unit map

- *To check for breadth*. Do you have a broad range of styles, genres and traditions? Do students have opportunities to engage with all the areas identified in the Range and Content and the Curriculum Opportunities sections of the Programme of Study? Are there sufficient opportunities for students to follow their own interests as part of the music curriculum? Is there a full range of teaching and learning styles – informal and formal; closed, guided and open; individual, small group and class ensemble? Do students have opportunities to be creative, generating unexpected outcomes?
- *To check for depth*. Is each unit placed at the appropriate point in terms of the stages of progression (outlined in Table 10.1)? Do the units gradually offer opportunities for students' work at the highest levels? How are the Key Processes developed throughout the scheme of work? For example, how will the expectations of ensemble skills in Year 9 be different from those expected in Year 7?

Finally, as you start to plan for individual lessons, you will need to consider how you can focus on developing the 'quality' of students' musical responses. This has been a focus of recent Ofsted judgements about music education.

> Work tended to focus on developing the students' technical competence without enough consideration of the quality of their musical response and the depth of musical understanding. (Ofsted 2009: 23)

One of the criteria for a judgement of 'good' music provision is described as:

> A constant emphasis on musical quality and aural development, and practical music-making helps learners learn how to respond musically. (Ofsted 2009: 72)

Summary

Having a clear concept of musical progression and development assists us in devising compelling learning experiences that are purposeful in helping students to demonstrate musical understanding. This chapter has presented a two-stage process to help develop an overview of the curriculum as a whole and then relate individual units of work to this through a consideration of the Key Concepts. It has emphasised that it is helpful to build links between different musical contexts, to ensure a range of coverage and an appropriate blend of each of the Key Processes of musical learning throughout. By placing the curriculum map overview at the centre of planning we have emphasised the importance of a balanced, rich and relevant curriculum to enable our learners to enjoy their experiences with us. The advantage of the planning tool is that the whole picture can be seen on one page. This gives you a clear map of where you are taking the students on their learning journeys.

Reflective Questions

1. Do my units of work build musical understanding progressively?
2. Are my units of work part of a broad, balanced and relevant music curriculum?
3. If units are planned at a particular stage of progression, how can I cater for those who are beyond or below that particular stage of musical attainment?
4. What can I do to offer a range of varied learning experiences?

Further Reading 

DfES (2006) *KS3 Music: A Professional Development Programme*, as revised DCSF (2008). Online at: http://www3.hants.gov.uk/music (accessed 21 November 2010).
Mills, J. (2005) *Music in the School*. Oxford: Oxford University Press (in particular Chapter 11: 'Making Progress in Music').

References

DfES (2006a) 'Unit 1: 'Structuring Learning for Musical Understanding', *KS3 Music: A Professional Development Programme*, as revised DCSF (2008). Online at: http://www3.hants.gov.uk/music/theunits/unit1.htm (accessed 16 February 2010).
DfES (2006b) 'Defining Musical Understanding Six Stages of Progression in Unit 5: Challenge in Music', *KS3 Music: A Professional Development Programme*, as revised DCSF (2008). Online at: http://www3.hants.gov.uk/r5d_definition_of_understanding_sheet_with_levels.pdf (accessed 21 November 2010).
DfES (2006c) 'Unit 1: Recognising Impact', *KS3 Music: A Professional Development Programme*, as received DCSF (2008). Online at: http://www3.hants.gov.uk/music/theunits/unit1/unit-objectives/unit-p2-recognisingimpact.htm (accessed 16 December 2010).
Ofsted (2009) *Making More of Music: An Evaluation of Music in Schools 2005/08*. London: Ofsted.
Philpott, C. (2007) 'Musical Learning', in C. Philpott and G. Spruce (eds), *Learning to Teach Music in the Secondary School: A Companion to School Experience* (2nd edn). Abingdon: Routledge.
Qualifications and Curriculum Authority (2007a) *Music: Programme of Study for Key Stage 3 and Attainment Target*. London: QCA.
Qualifications and Curriculum Authority (2007b) 'What has changed and why?' Online at: http://curriculum.qcda.gov.uk/uploads/overview_doc_tcm8-1839.pdf (accessed 16 December 2010).
Swanwick, K. (1979) *A Basis for Music Education*. Abingdon: Routledge.
Swanwick, K. (1999) *Teaching Music Musically*. Abingdon: Routledge.

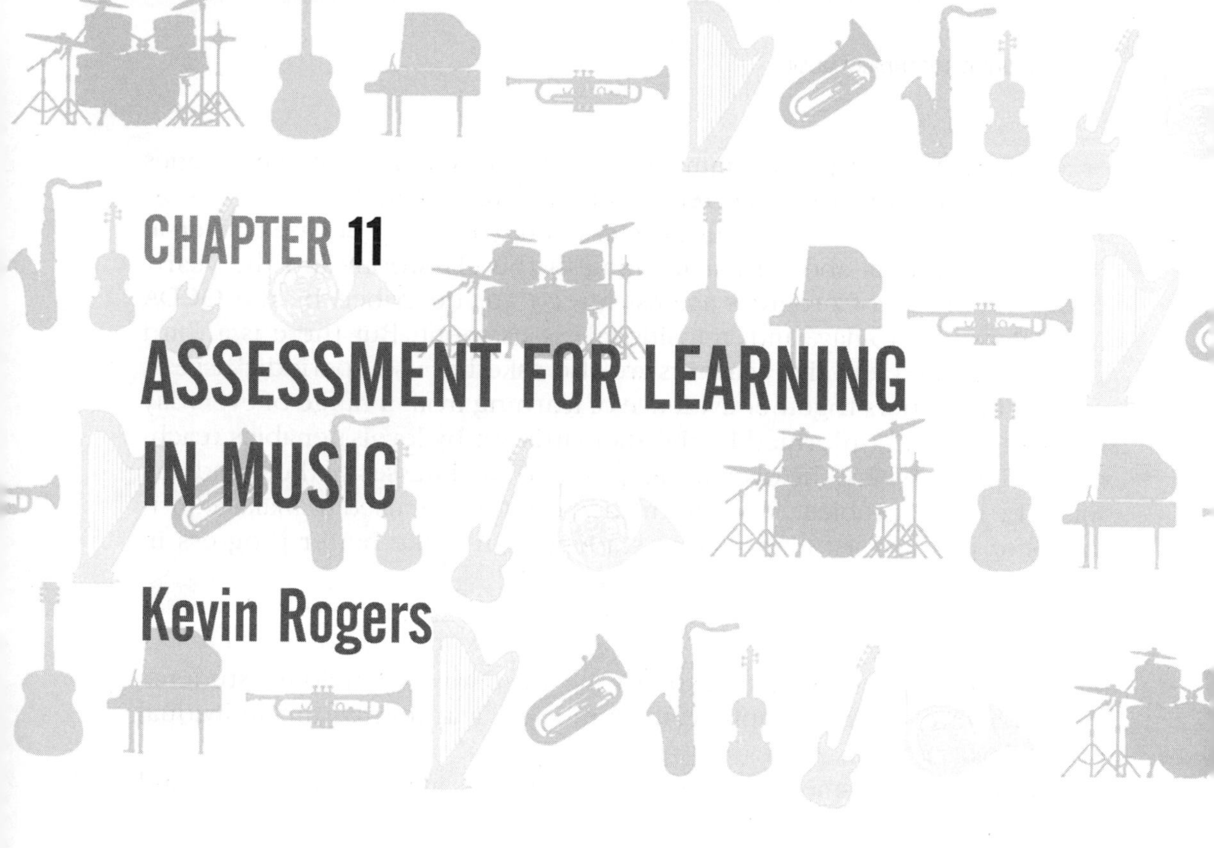

CHAPTER 11

ASSESSMENT FOR LEARNING IN MUSIC

Kevin Rogers

Introduction

Over the course of the past decade, much has been written about the use of assessment in the classroom. Most of it has been generic and has focused on Assessment for Learning (AfL) – a set of principles for daily assessment in the classroom that dramatically shifts the emphasis away from an external assessment by the teacher towards internal assessment by the student. But how do these principles apply to music? What are the implications for a subject in which planned learning is based primarily on a holistic approach to the subject, and in which the quality of musical processes is usually more significant than the quantity of students' technical output?

At the same time, the drive from school senior leadership teams to use National Curriculum levels as a tool for assessing and tracking progress has presented real problems for music teachers. We all know that levels are supposed to be end-of-Key-Stage assessments, summarising students' progress over two or three years of learning, and they do this job very well. Yet music teachers are often expected to use these levels within individual lessons, and to report progress every half term. Does this make sense of music learning, or are there better ways of summarising students' achievement over a series of lessons that more accurately reflect what we are looking for?

These two opposite extremes of assessment (the daily, private conversation with students about their learning in the classroom and the yearly public reporting of progress against levels) are described by the QCDA (2010a) as 'day-to-day' and 'transitional' assessment. But there is a third aspect of assessment that teachers are also asked to use: 'periodic' assessment. This gathers together evidence of learning from a range of everyday assessments and (informed by the standards set by levels) enables teachers to identify where the overall strengths and weaknesses of their students might be in their subject. This information can then be used to make adjustments to planned learning so that students can make better progress in the future.

In this chapter, we shall take each aspect of assessment in turn:

- day-to-day assessment to explore the best ways of helping students understand how to improve their musical learning within individual lessons;
- transitional assessment to explore what the levels in music really mean and the implications for assessment practice;
- periodic assessment to see how it can be informed by the levels, but can provide a much more detailed appraisal of your students' progress that will help develop your understanding of assessment for musical learning.

Day-to-day assessment

The recent emphasis on AfL means that most music teachers will know the principles of day-to-day assessment: the importance of explicit learning objectives and success criteria, questioning and dialogue, self- and peer-assessment, feedback, etc. The basic ideas will have been shaped locally by whole-school approaches and policies, and teachers will be required to demonstrate that these are being implemented in their own classrooms.

A useful way of finding out whether these principles are really operating in music is to invite a colleague to come into your lesson and ask the students some simple questions as they work. The questions and some typical answers outlined in Table 11.1 will enable you to judge whether the basic principles of effective day-to-day assessment are in place or not.

The effective responses show that the student:

- understands that the playing of the tune is important but that it is not the main point of the learning, which is about how blues tunes 'work'. This is

Table 11.1 Assessment for learning evaluation

Question	Typical response where day-to-day assessment is effective	Typical response where day-to-day assessment is not effective
'What are you doing?'	'Playing a blues tune'	'Playing a tune on the keyboard'
'Why are you doing it?'	'Because it helps us to learn about how tunes work in a typical 12-bar blues'	'Because the teacher told us to'
'Why are you doing the blues?'	'Because we are learning how blues music influenced later popular music styles'	'Don't know'
'What are you learning?'	'We are learning how to play with a blues feel'	'To play the tune'
'How will you get better?'	'By using better fingering so that we can get the blues notes more fluently'	'By practising'
'What will a good performance sound like?'	'One that is in time with the bass line, swings well and has a third line as fluent and accurate as the first two'	'Don't know – maybe to play the third line as well as the first two?'

critical: it demonstrates that the student understands the holistic nature of the subject, and recognises that the separate components (performing, composing, etc.) enable the development of musicianship and musical understanding;

- recognises how the learning in this lesson relates to the bigger picture of the whole unit;
- understands that 'getting better' is not determined by increasing technical complexity, but is actually determined by aspects of musical quality (being able to play more 'fluently');
- knows what 'good' sounds like – hopefully because the student has heard the teacher model it, has seen a video clip or has heard examples of previous students' work.

By contrast, the ineffective responses show that the student is simply engaged in a technical exercise with little awareness of what they might learn or how to improve.

So, how can we build towards effective responses to these questions? Good practice will ensure that:

- Learning objectives for lessons are clear and focused on developing students' musical understanding rather than the activities that the students will be engaged in.
- The learning objectives are made explicit for the students and are explored musically so that students understand them properly. They are related to the unit as a whole, so that students know how learning in that lesson relates to the bigger picture.
- Satisfactory, good and outstanding examples of outcomes are modelled, so that students understand how they can get better. Note that modelling is not the same as demonstrating – modelling is about 'thinking aloud' the

Table 11.2 Expectations of learning

Teacher-based expectation of learning	Level-based expectation of learning (Level 5)
You know how to improvise effective 2-bar answers to the tune's opening 'questions' in a 12-bar blues structure	You can improvise melodic and rhythmic structures within given structures

processes of learning rather than simply demonstrating what it is that students have to do. This also requires a portfolio and/or examples from the real musical world to be readily available so that students can hear, feel and see what 'good' sounds like.

- Teaching makes it clear that 'how to improve' is based upon quality as much as quantity. It is true that adding parts or playing more sections represents some kind of technical progress. However, students need to recognise that the simplest music can be created and played with a musicianship that indicates real quality – and that this quality is the key indicator of improvement in musical learning.
- Definitions of satisfactory/good/outstanding are not defined by levels within lessons or units, but by expectations of learning. As already indicated, levels are very good for indicating long-term achievement, but they are the wrong tool for day-to-day learning and assessment. By using teacher-defined expectations of learning, students will have a much clearer and precise understanding of how to improve.
- In the example shown in Table 11.2, students, using the teacher defined expectations, are able to identify much more precisely where they are in their learning and how to improve during the lesson.

Transitional assessment

This is a formal recognition of achievement: a public, summary judgement of students' achievement and progress, drawing upon a full and wide-ranging bank of evidence exemplifying the students' learning and practical outcomes. As such, it relates achievement to a fixed standard so that everyone knows and recognises the quality and the demand of the work completed. It is best done at the end of a year or key stage, since anything more frequent muddles transitional assessment (which is summative) with periodic assessment (which is formative, designed to analyse strengths/weaknesses, so that issues can be addressed and improved by the end of the year). At Key Stage 3, transitional assessment is described using the National Curriculum level descriptions, so it is important to understand how the levels are constructed in music and what they mean.

Levels in music – the importance of the first sentence

Music is unique among all National Curriculum subjects in having an initial sentence that encapsulates the complete standard for each level. In effect, it describes musical understanding or musicianship, which immediately indicates that the levels in music are about the quality of musical learning and not about a specific quantity of musical knowledge or technical proficiency.

The first sentence defines that musical understanding very clearly: it is about the 'ingredients' of music (defined as *devices*, *processes* and *conventions* respectively for levels 5, 6 and 7), and the context of the music being studied (*time*, *place*, *culture*). It also indicates that this should be learned and demonstrated practically (students *explore*) as well as being articulated through knowledge *of* the music (students *identify*). This of course links directly to the Programme of Study for Music and the Key Concepts of Critical Understanding (the knowledge of 'ingredients'), Cultural Understanding (the context) and the Integration of Practice (including the practical experience).

The first sentences also describe the core progression in musical learning. In fact, the first sentence by itself is all that is needed – the rest of each level statement merely supplements the first sentence, showing how students can develop and demonstrate their musicianship and musical understanding. All of the level statements refer to *identify* and *explore* (or, at the highest levels, *discriminate* or *exploit*) but the key markers for progression are presented in Table 11.3. These terms are labels to define the quality of understanding and musicianship at each level – so they are not really separate things but are the same thing described at various stages of 'demand' or 'difficulty'.

Note that there is no reference to technical skills in any of these opening sentences. Where there are references to practical skills in the later sentences, these describe how the overarching musical qualities are demonstrated; they are not

Table 11.3 Determining progression in the level descriptors

Level	Key phrase determining progression: *How music works*	Key phrase determining progression: *The context*
4	'the relationship between sounds'	'how music reflects different intentions'
5	'musical devices'	'how music reflects time, place and culture
6	'different processes'	'contexts of selected musical styles, genres and traditions'
7	'musical conventions'	'influences on selected musical styles, genres and traditions'

Adapted from QCA (2007: 86–7).

intended as 'tick boxes' in their own right to indicate the achievement any particular 'level' in the student who demonstrates them. This means that there is no such thing as a 'level 5 performance': there is performing which reveals level 5 understanding and musicianship, but this is to do with how it reveals the student's understanding of devices and context, not about technical details regarding how many parts the student can play. As we have argued throughout this book, it is not appropriate to assess the Key Processes separately, as the students are developing their musical understanding in an integrated, holistic way.

Levels in music – other issues

Students need to demonstrate their musical learning across a range of styles, genres and traditions. QCDA (2010a) state that:

> A range of experiences is essential for attainment at all levels. Understanding of a variety of genres, styles and traditions is also essential for attainment especially above level 4. Attainment at the higher levels is impossible without depth and breadth of musical study and experience.

This is because the quality of musical thinking and musicianship is best revealed when it can be applied in different musical contexts – but again, this emphasises the point that progression in musical learning is about quality of understanding, not merely about technical proficiency.

A range of evidence types is also required:

> In planning units of work and classroom approaches, you will need to provide opportunities for students to display their achievements in different ways, and to work in a range of situations. (QCDA 2010a)

For Key Stage 3, as we have discussed, this also now includes performance in contexts within and beyond the classroom, developing performance skills which include the use of music technology and working with a range of musicians.

Progression in quality within a level is as important as the progression between levels: QCDA describes this as being a question of the 'increasing confidence, ownership and independence of the student' (QCDA 2010a). This is very different from specially written 'sub-level' statements which we believe should not be used under any circumstance.

Levels are not designed for single pieces of work:

> You will arrive at judgements by taking into account strengths and weaknesses in performance across a range of contexts and over a period of time, rather than focusing on a single piece of work. A single piece of work will not cover all the expectations set out in a level description. (QCDA 2010a)

Implications for assessment practice

As secure judgement for a level in music requires evidence from a range of styles/genres/traditions (which is highly unlikely to be met within one unit), it makes it impossible to say after one half-term that a student is 'at' a particular level. This means that half-termly 'levelling' in music is unrealistic. Our experience suggests that it is difficult to determine secure evidence for a level until at least three units of work have been completed. This might be possible to achieve after six months, but given the richness of learning implied by the Programme of Study, annual levelling would seem to be better.

This also means that levels should not be used as the basis for a single unit of work's assessment criteria. A unit's learning may be pitched at a certain level and should be informed by national expectations of musical learning. However, the detailed learning statements for the unit can only *contribute to* the developing sense of 'levelness': they cannot, on their own, *define* 'levelness' (i.e. specific singing skills cannot of themselves be fixed as 'level 5'). Therefore unit assessment criteria should be defined as 'expectations of learning': what it is that the teacher determines as being appropriate for that unit, given the planned learning already identified and recognising that understanding/musicianship and quality of music-making should be given the highest priority.

In particular, levels should not be used to describe gradations of technical difficulty: Ofsted in the *Making More of Music* report identified weak assessment practice in which

> ... students were told: 'Level 3: clap a 3-beat ostinato; Level 4: maintain a 4-bar ostinato; Level 5: compose an ostinato.' This demonstrated a significant misunderstanding of the expectations inherent in the level descriptions. (Ofsted 2009: 31)

Finally, we suggest that sub-levels should be focused on the increasing confidence, ownership and independence of the students. As suggested earlier, teachers can of course develop their own expectations of learning for practical work, but rather than defining arbitrary notions of sub-level progress, these should be designed to support understanding and contribute to an awareness of 'levelness' which is built up over a longer period of time.

Music teachers therefore need an alternative to the use of levels and so-called sub-levels to track progress over the course of the year. This leads us to our final assessment form, periodic assessment.

Periodic assessment

This is a term which describes how teachers can stand back from the details of day-to-day assessment and by looking at a range of evidence of learning identify where students' strengths/weaknesses are across the music curriculum as a whole. They can then make adjustments to teaching in order to improve the quality of students' musical learning as they work towards the end of the year/point of transition.

Periodic assessment is therefore primarily a tool for teachers: information may be shared with students and school managers, but it is designed to help teachers identify where developing strengths and weaknesses are, especially so that adaptations to teaching and the curriculum can be made to address identified areas of weakness.

Periodic assessment must also be informed by national expectations, since these define the expected standards. As QCDA states:

> Criteria should be grounded in the national curriculum programmes of study and level descriptions and should help to clarify progression within the subject or area. (QCDA 2010b)

The recently published *Exemplification for Foundation Subjects* (QCDA 2010c) provides clear guidance on national expectations.

Periodic assessment for music: evidence banks

The exemplification materials show the range of evidence that can be used to inform periodic assessments, but in music, the sheer number of students taught means that banks of audio or other evidence for every student cannot be created – it would be impossible. However, by use of sampling techniques, teachers can check their periodic judgements against national norms and use the process to inform their assessments of individual students whose work they see lesson by lesson. So, if a teacher realises that the sample indicates their assessments of overall understanding were too generous, they can apply that knowledge when they next see evidence of learning from another student whose work was not in the sample.

There are two sorts of sampling methods:

1. Select a small number of students, and focus only on these students, collecting a range of evidence from them over the course of two or three units of work, using these to test out the periodic assessments.
2. Collect evidence from any number of students, deliberately capturing in the process a range of satisfactory/good/outstanding work over time. This work is then periodically assessed: does it fit with the national exemplification of satisfactory/good/outstanding? are there particular areas of strength/weakness across the evidence as a whole? and so on.

Implications for the department

Music departments need to create a portfolio of work:

- For each unit of work, with evidence of learning which demonstrates how well students are progressing.
- Using final, end-of-unit 'performances' as part of the portfolio, but also a range of other types of evidence – completed plans, worksheets, scores (where appropriate), evaluations, 'before and after' recordings of the same piece to demonstrate capacity for refinement, etc.
- With all the evidence categorised into three groups. These should follow the example on the exemplification of standards site, so there should be evidence to demonstrate:

  (a) understanding the nature of music (understanding devices, processes, conventions and contexts);
  (b) communicating through creative music-making (all of singing, improvising, solo and ensemble performing, composing, arranging, etc.);
  (c) evaluating and informing practice (identifying, refining and evaluating, and using those skills to improve practical work and improve overall musical understanding).

These groups of evidence relate very clearly to specific aspects of the level statements. The learning they show can therefore also contribute to an eventual transitional assessment, as follows:

- 'understanding the nature of music' relates to the first sentence of the level statements;
- 'communicating through creative music-making' relates to those sentences in the level statements that show how practical work demonstrates musical understanding;
- 'evaluating and informing practice' relates to those sentences in the level statements that refer to listening, but also includes the additional capacity to use reviewing and evaluating to refine practical work and improve understanding.

It is critical to note, however, that the most significant aspects of evidence are those relating to 'understanding'; this evidence determines the overall quality and standard of work, to which the other aspects simply contribute.

By comparing this portfolio with the national examples, teachers should be able to:

- moderate their judgements against the national expectations;
- identify where there might be department-wide issues (e.g. 'generally weak evaluating') and then make changes to the curriculum/teaching in order to address them;

- support individual students where there is evidence in the portfolio of particular need.

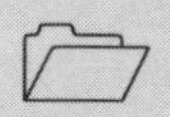

Developing periodic assessment

In a one-person department, the teacher decided to start the process of developing periodic assessment systems. She hoped that this would enable her to identify overall strengths and weaknesses in her students' learning and benchmark their work against national expectations.

She started by revising her planned learning for a Year 8 unit of work on film music, making sure that key learning was categorised into three areas: understanding, communicating through creative music-making, and evaluating and informing practice. Expectations of learning for each of these were defined using the model from Unit 1 of the Secondary Strategy website (http://www.ks3music.org.uk). Criteria for assessment were based on upon these expectations, and were shared with students so that they fully understood both the learning and the challenge that was being set.

The teacher identified six students: two each who she thought were likely to develop learning that was at, above or well above expectations. Over the course of the unit, she tried to note when each of these students demonstrated learning of a particular quality for each of the three main areas. In addition, she noted in her mark book if any of the students produced work that was surprising in some way. At the end of the unit, she made sure that she had as much evidence as was reasonably possible to capture – worksheets, written evaluations and audio recordings, both of 'work in progress' that she asked the students to make, and the final, end-of-unit performances. She then made a final decision on what standard of learning each student had demonstrated by the end of the unit for each of the three main areas of learning.

Although she recognised that the evidence of learning from one unit would be limited, she decided to compare what she had with the exemplification examples (QCDA 2010c). By comparing the evidence of learning she had with the range of evidence demonstrated on the website, she recognised that her students had not really been able to demonstrate clear learning in the area of musical understanding – particularly in the way that context can affect the way music is created and performed. She therefore revisited her draft planning for the next unit to enable greater exploration of this crucial aspect of musical learning.

At the same time, she began to get a better feel for the overall standard of the work being produced by her students. Although she recognised that evidence from one unit could not indicate an overall level, she decided that her expectations for

(Continued)

(Continued)

these Year 8 students were appropriate, as they seemed to be comparable with the evidence shown for level 5. She planned to revisit the comparison after two further units (on samba and folk music), hoping to see greater evidence for musical understanding and a more secure judgement on the overall standard of her students' work.

Tracking students' progress

All of this implies very regular use of audio and/or video recording. It also requires a way of logging significant other evidence, even if this only means a note for the teacher as a reminder rather than a recording or copy of the actual work itself.

Departments need something, therefore, which enables the following:

- Day-to-day jottings, with evidence of learning from individual lessons which may contribute to periodic assessments. These will not be for every student in every lesson, but will identify evidence of learning which is surprising or in some other way notable (e.g. a student who is normally underconfident performs with flair and fluency).
- Judgements about the three main aspects of learning (understanding, music-making and evaluating) for every student across every unit. These will include end-of-unit outcomes, and evidence collected as the unit progresses (e.g. a comment a student made during the planning/exploration phase of practical work which indicated a very clear understanding of the context and purpose of the music). This is not therefore just about marking end-of-unit performances: though these may contribute evidence for any one of the three main areas, it is important to be gathering evidence of musical learning across the whole unit.

If these judgements are captured consistently over a period of time, they will of course begin to demonstrate progress. The judgements against the main unit criteria will give the strongest indicators of progress, but these should be refined by reference to the day-to-day jottings and any other knowledge of the students' musical interests such as involvement in bands or ensembles. When there is sufficient information from a range of work, the sequence of judgements can eventually provide indicative information about a likely 'level' for transitional assessment purposes. However, it is crucial to reinforce the point that for day-to-day and periodic assessment, the teacher's expectations of learning (as described in planned learning, including the criteria for assessment based upon those expectations) will provide the most accurate and meaningful indicators of progress in musical learning.

An example of one solution to this process can be found at http://www3.hants.gov.uk/hms-ks3-assessment.htm

Summary

Assessment of musical learning requires a direct connection with planning, learning (musical understanding, knowledge of music and practical experience, all informed by contextual awareness) and a focus on overall quality. This will avoid an overemphasis on fragmented aspects of musical techniques and knowledge, and instead provide a holistic approach to musical learning and its assessment.

Reflective Questions

1. Do I practise effective day-to-day assessment using explicit expectations of learning which develop students' understanding of how to improve?
2. Is my transitional assessment based on a secure knowledge of students' musical understanding and their learning across a range of styles, genres and traditions?
3. How can I develop a range of evidence to underpin periodic assessment to support the ongoing development of effective teaching and learning?
4. How can I track students' progress within the three main aspects of learning – understanding the nature of music; communication through creative music-making and evaluating and informing practice?

Further Reading

DCSF (2006) *KS3 Music: A Professional Development Programme.* www.ks3music.org.uk (accessed 21 November 2010).

Fautley, M. (2010) *Assessment in Music Education*. Oxford: Oxford University Press.

References

Ofsted (2009) *Making More of Music: An Evaluation of Music in Schools 2005/08*. London: Ofsted.

Qualifications and Curriculum Authority (2007) *Music: Programme of Study for Key Stage 3 and Attainment Target*. London: QCA.

Qualifications and Curriculum Development Agency (2010a) *Assessment in Music* http://curriculum.qcda.gov.uk/key-stages-1-and-2/assessment/assessmentofsubjects/assessmentin-music/index.aspx (accessed 21 November 2010).
Qualifications and Curriculum Development Agency (2010b) *Periodic Assessment* http://curriculum.qcda.gov.uk/key-stages-3-and-4/assessment/assessment_and_curriculum/day-to-day-periodic-and-transitional-assessment/Periodic/index.aspx (accessed 21 November 2010).
Qualifications and Curriculum Development Agency (2010c) *Exemplification for Foundation Subjects* http://curriculum.qca.org.uk/key-stages-3and4/assessment/exemplification/index.aspx (accessed 21 November 2010).

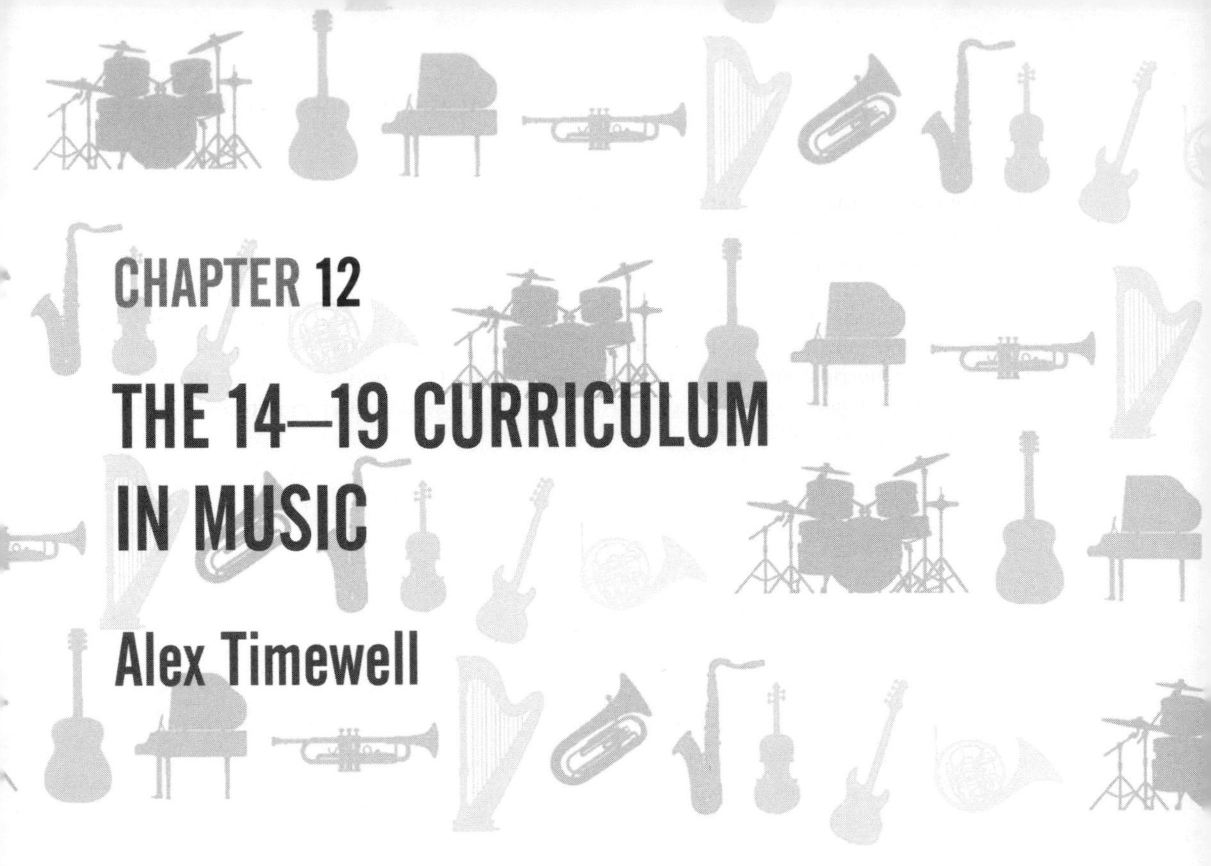

CHAPTER 12

THE 14–19 CURRICULUM IN MUSIC

Alex Timewell

Introduction

The 14–19 curriculum structures students' progression from school into the wider world. At this important moment in life, young people are developing the awareness and skills they need to operate in the complexity of demanding and difficult social environments. The ability to adjust from dependency on the structure school provides to independent members of the community is vital to successful integration into an adult world.

The music curriculum can provide a very useful context for facilitating this progression as learners can explore ways of expressing their creative and cultural identities, developing outlets for their personal opinions and methods to articulate their feelings. Music-making also involves using important transferable skills – communication, team working, presentation, project management and problem-solving – that are essential in many aspects of life. As we have suggested throughout this book, when focused on music-making, students display such skills without them appearing onerous or in anyway abstracted from the musical goals they are trying to achieve.

The aim of this chapter is to reflect on ways in which you can help students develop their musical identity, encourage them to think about their learning and take ownership over their music-making activities. If students can begin to identify their own goals and take responsibility for realising them, they will be better prepared for the world they progress onto. The traditional GCSE and A level qualifications now compete with a range of alternatives that are focused on developing skills that will be useful in industrial practice and for future workers in the knowledge economy. Here, music must be seen as an essential cultural ingredient that cannot be described as a particular set of styles and methods, but a potential range of different social activities each with their own historical practices and meanings.

Guiding principles

This chapter outlines four guiding principles for music teachers working in the 14–19 curriculum. These guiding principles take account of the diversity of musical cultures that young people may bring to the classroom. Balancing the demands of conservatoire methods often found in syllabi with the alternative traditions found in other cultures is fundamental to successful delivery in the 14–19 curriculum. Keeping the students interested, making the curriculum relevant and ensuring that students learn prescribed skills requires a critical approach to curriculum design as well as knowledge of a broad range of musical styles and techniques. However, no one teacher can be expected to have expertise in all the musical styles and cultures they need to work with. The challenge of coping with the familiar and unfamiliar while encouraging students to gain confidence and independence is the focus of these guiding principles.

Ownership of learning

Who has control over learning? Who should have control? The relationship between teacher and students will be affected by how this question might be answered. If the students are allowed control over what they learn, they may choose not to apply themselves to difficult tasks, they may get distracted or they may set themselves goals that are inappropriate or unrealistic. Students need a teacher. However, if the teacher has complete control over what students learn, the students may not engage with or really understand what they are supposed to be learning.

The relevance of the curriculum to students is important. Socio-cultural relevance can mean a number of things including:

- progression – if a student intends to continue with music as a career and how they conceive this career evolving;
- cultural influences – the musical values and tastes they bring with them to the classroom;
- social life – how they may use music to engage in social interactions with friends.

Each student will bring his or her own interests and understandings of music.

Metal versus R & B

Different combinations of students can result in a wide range of stylistic preferences and cultural influences in any one class. However, the possible divisions that may be perceived by students working together can be used for a positive outcome. A typical scenario may involve a band containing several male guitarists who like to play Heavy Metal and several female vocalists who like to sing R & B. The construction of gender and race in musical discourse is evident here but does not necessarily limit the opportunities for students to develop as musicians.

The desire to make music can often overcome any reluctance students may have to engage with each other because of their apparent differences. They often decide to compromise, either by taking it in turns to learn a piece of music in each style or by creating a new composition that uses elements of each style. Another strategy is to ask the students to work instead on a song in a style of music that is not to any one student's particular taste, but one which is historically and musically relevant to each student's cultural influences. In this way they are encouraged to think creatively beyond the bounds of their current knowledge, they learn from each other and gain satisfaction from their growing musicianship that is manifest in the work they produce.

The difficult task of allowing for the diverse interests and skills of a class and also ensuring they can present evidence that they have achieved the skills that are required in the syllabus is a major concern of teachers delivering the 14–19 curriculum. As students progress, they will want to take increasing amounts of control over their work. There are various ways that a teacher can facilitate developing ownership and decision-making while guiding learning into productive activities, but they all involve a sense of collaboration, cooperation and trust in the student–teacher relationship. Success will involve taking an interest in students' attitudes to music and exploring the musical material that they bring to the classroom. The teacher will need to exemplify how different musical styles and music-making activities can be evidenced in relation to assessment criteria.

Building knowledge and skills

As well as building a sense of their own style and identity as a musician, students also need to be able to access other musicians' knowledge and develop the skills to communicate with them. They need to be able to make critical judgements about the tools and methods they use, while analysing and synthesising their experiences with the musical materials they encounter. It is the task of the music teacher to create opportunities for students to take an interest in music-making activities that will require them to engage in the key processes that are central to independent music-makers. It is important for the music teacher to provide a safe environment in which students can experiment and explore different ways of expressing their ideas. But it is also important for a balanced range of well-established musical devices to be introduced to students to ensure they can develop the ability to understand and communicate with other musicians in a range of different environments.

Clapping rhythms

Students will often focus on particular aspects of musicianship, developing knowledge of scales and harmony or becoming engaged with music theory in an abstract manner, without really understanding them through application in their performance. In one school, rhythmic awareness exercises are used to build students' performance techniques. Such exercises, which involve walking on the spot, counting and clapping out rhythms, are useful in a number of different ways. Firstly, they introduce the sense of physicality of performance. When a musician plays they use the whole of their body to perform and this is visible to the audience. Frequently students can be seen performing music but looking uncomfortable on stage; this indicates a tension that can be seen as a lack of movement or inability to look up from their instrument. Secondly, clapping rhythms helps bring a focus on the rhythmic nature of music and can be used to explain why an understanding of rhythm is as fundamentally important as knowledge of scales and harmony. Finally, clapping rhythms is a good opportunity to explore and explain some of the theoretical conventions associated with understanding and notating harmony. A whiteboard is used to notate rhythms being played or to let the students take turns at writing rhythms to perform.

Activities need to be prescribed and controlled, but each with sufficient time and opportunity for students to participate in a way that is meaningful to them. Without a sense of why an activity is useful to them or how it connects with their personal goals and current skills, they may become frustrated and disengaged. Harder to deal with than a disengaged student is a student that absorbs information and can follow instruction but does not see the value in experimentation. Such a student may be able to identify the key processes that are important to music-making but will struggle to take a critical view or to synthesise or evaluate the materials they encounter or create. Faced with a class with a range of musical ability and stylistic interests, the music teacher's task becomes a balancing act. Fortunately, enthusiastic and engaged students are important contributors to the development of the musical skills and knowledge of the whole class – their individual experiences and knowledge of a range of music is often invaluable!

Differentiation and personalisation

Some examples of the kinds of activities that facilitate students' personal exploration in a class context could include large-scale projects like planning a musical performance, preparing recordings for an album, composing music for a particular purpose or researching musical tastes and experiences. Each of these activities requires students to work in a focused and collaborative way, but also allows for each class member to take on different levels of responsibility, bring their own tastes and opinions to the project, produce different types of musical materials and engage with other people's ideas. The role of the teacher is to stimulate the students' enthusiasm by clearly presenting the project, its relevance, the expected musical goals and the opportunities for each student to learn and share with others.

Smaller tasks can also take on a similar role in developing the students' learning. Presenting one element of a musical process to engage and experiment with can also lead to discrete and measurable activities that are possible for each student to make their own.

Composition sketchbook

With a Year 10 group, a teacher uses a composition sketchbook to develop students' understanding of music theory and harmony. Each week a simple theoretical aspect is introduced such as a dynamics, rhythmic cells, binary form or the major triad, exploring with the class different possibilities for its use, methods for notation and ways of communicating these ideas. The teacher models how to create a little compositional idea using simple rules that limit the scope of what can be produced. Examples might be a two-bar baseline or perhaps a simple melody for a flute to accompany the chords to 'Wild Thing', articulated in formal and practical forms of notation. These are then performed by the teacher or some of the students. Following on from this, the students are asked to create their own compositional ideas and to notate them so that they may be performed at the end of the lesson. Students keep their ideas in a sketchbook which can be used as stimulus material in longer pieces.

During this process, students develop the ability to communicate their ideas explicitly in writing and for a specific audience – other musicians. In recognising the need for common languages with which musicians can express their ideas to each other, students are able to take ownership of theoretical and notational methods that are often taught in an abstract manner, divorced from the processes of composing and performing. The important thing here is that students are free to experiment. Over a unit of work, each student generates a wealth of ideas, knowledge and skills that they can use as a resource for future in-depth compositional work. It also provides sufficient evidence of each student's understanding, use and application of the theoretical and notational skills that are required by the syllabus they are working to.

Working with a syllabus

Music teachers will always have a prescribed set of goals to work towards. Assessment criteria and learning outcomes are given for the teacher to design a curriculum that is appropriate to a particular class of students. The level and form of prescription may vary depending on the particular qualification or syllabus they are using; how the curriculum is designed will be dependent on the skills and contexts of the students they are teaching. These factors will inform the choice of qualification a teacher or music department may choose to employ.

The required evidence trail that constitutes the assessment process can appear onerous and intimidating to many new teachers. Reading a syllabus for the first time, the teacher is confronted with a range of requirements that may seem bewildering and disconnected from musicians' practice. To account for the growing recognition of the varying cultural contexts in which music education is delivered, many syllabi have introduced a level of ambiguity to their assessment criteria, making them process driven and open to a diversity of musical content. This is a real advantage for confident music teachers, creating the space for them to negotiate their own strengths and musical skills into the curriculum, as well as providing flexibility for the implementation of a range of assessment devices.

However, this ambiguity can create uncertainty for the less confident music teacher. Syllabi will often provide suggested content, ideas for curriculum design and appropriate methods of assessment, and a rationale explaining the intended purpose of the unit. These should be read and considered carefully; they often provide a catalyst for designing the curriculum and writing schemes of work, lesson plans and delivery materials. It is important to recognise which parts of a syllabus are prescribed and which are suggested.

Rehearsal logs

In the case of our band of Heavy Metal guitarists and R & B singers, their course – the Edexcel BTEC Level 3 Diploma – allows much of the evidence needed to demonstrate their learning to be generated during the course of their planning and rehearsing. The Unit 22: Music Performance Session Styles learning outcome 22.3 states: 'Students must be able to apply stylistically accurate elements to a range of musical genres in different performance situations'. This outcome can be evidenced in a variety of ways; perhaps the most obvious is through the use of a rehearsal log where students reflect in writing at the end of each rehearsal on what they have achieved. However, other materials generated can also go a long way in providing the evidence they need: chord charts, lyrics, bar counts, parts for different instruments, songs they have listened to, sleeve notes, Internet searches, flyers or posters they create to advertise their gigs, Myspace, Facebook or Reverbnation profiles and so on. Observational evidence can also be used, as well as video or audio recordings, notes from peer discussions or tutor comments and feedback.

External verifiers often appreciate seeing samples of delivery materials and student work that is innovative, unusual and creative. Clearly stated assessment criteria mean that at all times the assessment is transparent and reasonable decisions can be made. It is possible over a period of several years to build a good relationship with verifiers who will usually appreciate sincere engagement with the syllabus and will construct their criticism to ensure that the teacher's awareness of any issues with delivery are reflected upon and improved in future years. Ultimately curriculum design must be seen as an evolving and reflective process that requires critical judgement from the teacher and willingness to share good practice.

Examples from the classroom

The guiding principles outlined above need careful consideration when designing an appropriate 14–19 music curriculum. A young person's development will benefit from a:

- growing sense of ownership of the activities they participate in;
- base of knowledge and skills that is culturally sensitive but also forges an identification with musicianship and the practice of other musicians;
- recognition that each student is an individual who has their own set of goals and understandings of what music is;
- framework within which to develop and evaluate their progress.

The job of the music teacher may therefore seem to be complicated. It can be intimidating to be presented with range of students with different skill levels, stylistic influences and cultural backgrounds and deliver a music curriculum that ensures they all progress in their music-making activities, evidenced to specific criteria in a given syllabus. A traditional model may involve an expectation that particular skills and repertoire be developed, but in this chapter we have advocated a student-centred approach to the 14–19 curriculum with an expectation that students will provide a proportion of the content and direction of the curriculum. When students are allowed to express their own expertise, the authority of the music teacher may become endangered, affecting their ability to manage the classroom environment and ensure that the syllabus requirements are met. However, if the teacher engages in negotiation with their class, all participants can feel valued and engaged in positive music-making. Careful and creative curriculum design can provide a framework and a safe environment for this to happen. The following case studies give examples of how this might work in practice.

Learning lists

In many syllabi, the music teacher is responsible for developing the performance skills of their students. This requires consideration of a range of factors: instrumental skill, knowledge of a range of styles, selection and rehearsal techniques, consideration of audience, emotional aspects of performance, ownership and interpretation of material, communication and stagecraft, etc. To manage the factors, one strategy is to introduce a 'learning list' of pieces, from which the students, working in ensembles, have to choose four to work on.

(Continued)

(Continued)

A learning list is a good way to balance the differing agendas of students and teachers in the classroom. It gives the students some ownership of the material they will use but it ensures that the teacher can include a variety of different styles and challenging material appropriate to build students' repertoire and musical knowledge. Importantly, it helps students begin to develop a sense of responsibility for the choices they make and consider the different requirements different musical material demands of a musician. The different approaches to performing demanded by each piece will require the student to think about their musicianship in slightly different ways building an identifiable set of skills and broadening their knowledge of a range of musical styles.

Furthermore, students can use this as a model for future practice. It is unlikely that students will be satisfied working entirely from material chosen by the teacher – they will have their own opinions and tastes in music and will want to express themselves by selecting their own material. Suggesting they brainstorm a range of ideas for material to develop and narrowing it down to a shortlist by using self-devised criteria that are appropriate to what they are trying to achieve is a process that is versatile and effective. It also allows the teacher to become familiar with the students' own tastes and what they enjoy in music. This can be an enriching experience for the teacher.

Working on a groove – 'Funky Kingston'

Fundamental to engaging students is their sense of being successful in the tasks they are set. Often this is not an easy task when the class has a range of students with different skills, aptitudes and abilities. Using musical material as a common resource for a class of students to work on together and develop their skills can be approached in a number of different ways. The author has used an arrangement of 'Funky Kingston' by Toots & the Maytals available on http://jsavage.org.uk/wp-content/uploads/2011/03/Funky-Kingston-Full-Score-1.pdf as a basis for developing differentiated ensemble work in the classroom.

This piece has a number of advantages. It is a style of music that many students may have an opinion about but probably not a particular allegiance to or against. Having been used as a soundtrack to a number of television advertisements over the past couple of years it may also be somewhat familiar to them. It is also a good example of the way popular music can demonstrate

(Continued)

(Continued)

unconventional use of harmony; the guitar plays G minor harmony at the same time the keyboard plays G major harmony. This apparent dissonance creates tension and energy in the song, a point probably worth saving for more advanced students.

The complexity of the rhythmic interaction between instruments is contrasted by the relative simplicity of each individual part. The melodic parts are interchangeable allowing for a range of instrumentalists to participate in a performance and each part has a different challenge. Key to understanding this is the rhythmic and melodic movement. The underlying groove can be seen in the left-hand keyboard part, playing the role of the bassline as the bass guitar has a lead melody role to perform. Beginners should be given this to work on first. More able students may try the guitar part or right-hand keyboard part. The drum part is simple but not intuitive to many musicians: it is essential that drummers listen to the track carefully to try and imitate the length of the 'skip' – alternate quavers are played strong then soft and this cannot be notated precisely. The bassline requires an instrumentalist who has some real control over their phrasing and an adequate level of rhythmic understanding and technique.

Each phrase can be applied independently, supplying stimuli for experimentation and developing motivic phrases, particularly through its use of pentatonics, repetition and syncopation.

Summary

When designing and teaching a music curriculum for 14–19 year olds, it is important to recognise the key role that music plays in their developing identities as young adults and independent learners preparing to enter the wider world. Encouraging students to build musical knowledge and skills must be balanced with providing them with an opportunity to take ownership over their learning. This will mean that their musical tastes and stylistic interests need to be given space for expression while providing a framework against which they can reflect on their learning.

A creative approach to curriculum design can be enriching and rewarding for music teachers as well. Using a sense of shared musicianship to find commonalities with students enables the teacher to understand and value their opinions, and teaching and learning to become activities that both teacher engage in. The authenticity and variety of material produced in the classroom through composition and performance will be greatly enhanced.

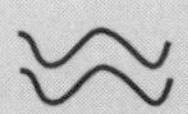

Reflective Questions

1. What resources do my students bring to the class? How can their knowledge and enthusiasm be encouraged and shared?
2. What opportunities can be created through structured processes to explore how individuals identify with music and use music to express their identity?
3. What materials generated through music-making processes can be collected and presented as evidence of learning to meet syllabus requirements?

Further Reading

Crow, B. (2006) 'Musical creativity and the new technology', *Music Education Research*, 8(1): 121–30.

Green, L. (2006) 'Popular music education in and for itself, and for "other" music: current research in the classroom', *International Journal of Music Education*, 24(2): 101–18.

O'Flynn, J. (2005) 'Re-appraising ideas of musicality in intercultural contexts of music education', *International Journal of Music Education*, 23(3): 191–203.

Regelski, T. (2007) '"Music teacher" – meaning and practice, identity and position', *Action, Criticism and Theory for Music Education*, 6(2): 1–35.

References

Edexcel (2009) *BTEC Level 3 Diploma in Music (QCF)*. Online at: http://www.edexcel.com/quals/nationals10/music/ (accessed 1 October 2010).

Timewell, A. (2010) (Arr.) 'Funky Kingston' – Toots & The Maytals. Online at: www.jsavage.org.uk (accessed 30 November 2010).

INDEX

Added to a page number 'f' denotes a figure and 't' denotes a table.